SPITTING IMAGE

by

SHUTTA CRUM

CLARION BOOKS
NEW YORK

Clarion Books
a Houghton Mifflin Company imprint
215 Park Avenue South, New York, NY 10003
Copyright © 2003 by Shutta Crum

The text was set in 12.5-point Carre Noir Light.

www.houghtonmifflinbooks.com

Printed in the U.S.A.

Library of Congress Cataloging-in-Publication Data
Crum, Shutta.
Spitting image / by Shutta Crum.
p.   cm.
Summary: In the small town of Baylor, Kentucky, twelve-year-old Jessie K. Bovey and her
friends confront some of life's questions during their summer vacation in the late 1960s.
ISBN 0-618-23477-2 (alk. paper)
[1. Family life—Kentucky—Fiction. 2. Fathers—Fiction.
3. Friendship—Fiction. 4. Kentucky—History—20th century—Fiction.] I. Title.
PZ7.C888288 Sp 2003
[Fic]—dc21   2002015912

QUM 10 9 8 7 6 5 4 3 2

For my sister, Brenda (Crum) Proos, with love

acknowledgments

This book could not have come about without the support and honest criticism of the following people: my good friends Ruth Haldeman, Susan Livingston, and librarian extraordinaire Paula Schaffner; my hard-working and supportive critique group—B.J. Connor, Gail Flynn, Tracy Gallup, Mary Lind, Ginny Ryan, Nancy Shaw, Debbie Taylor, Shanda Trent, Hope Vestergaard, and Joan Weisman; my young critical readers— Lydia Aikenhead, Anna Flynn, Emilie Flynn, Alec Lind, Anna Lind, Ian Lind, and Rebecca Schaffner; Dr. Marvin Meyer, DVM; my loving and confident family, who never doubted that this book would come to be, especially my husband, Gerald Clark, and my parents, Melvin and Evelyn Crum, who helped me with many of the details of country life in Kentucky; and editor Dinah Stevenson, who took the leap of faith.

one

I SAT IN FRONT of the hardware store eating ice cream with my best friends, Robert Ketchum and his little brother, Baby Blue. The sidewalk dipped, and the window ledge was the perfect spot to plop down, stretch out our legs, and rest our feet.

It was less than two miles into Hiram from where we lived in Baylor. We had walked into town to buy the cones. It was my treat. I'd saved up sixty-five cents from helping my good friend and neighbor, Lester, at the filling station he owned in Baylor, the Gas & Go. When we got to Hiram, we had headed straight for the Dixie Dairy Delight, next door to the hardware store.

Mmm! We barely spoke, eating up that good cold vanilla ice cream. Missy Salyer, who I used to be in Girl Scouts with, called out, "Hi, Jessie," as she rode her bike by. Lorelei McMasters and DeeDee Byrum passed without so much as a nod. Lorelei's father is the mayor of Hiram and DeeDee's father is the banker. Neither one's got a sociable bone in her body, unless you're a boy and happen to be named Billy Lee Wells or Brian Holcum.

Robert and Baby Blue hardly even looked up as Lorelei and DeeDee went by. I stuck my chin out as far as I could and took a great big tongueful of vanilla ice cream and let it sit there in plain sight, for just a moment longer than necessary.

"Ugh!" Lorelei shuddered.

"Grow up," I heard DeeDee mutter.

Suddenly, I noticed something different about both of them. Since school had let out last month, they'd grown bosoms.

"Did you see that?" I whispered to Robert. "Miss Stuck-Up and Junior Miss Stuck-Up have grown—out in front."

Robert looked, but they'd already gone by. "What d'you mean?" he asked.

"Booo-zums," I drawled, like the boys from school did. "Big ones."

Robert looked again, shrugged, and went back to his ice cream cone.

"So..." I nudged him with my elbow.

"So?" he asked.

"So they've got to be fake. Isn't that disgusting?"

"Hmm," he replied, licking his fingers and neatly dabbing at his chin with a paper napkin. "I don't care what Lorelei and DeeDee do."

I swear, even though Robert and I have been friends since we were little babies, sometimes he just makes me want to scream, especially when all he seems to be interested in is what's going on in his own head. "Don't you care when someone's being a big fat faker?" I asked him.

That was when I saw that wrinkled-up, hard-thinking

2

look on his face that he gets sometimes. "What?" I asked, throwing my hands up in the air. "What?"

"Just trying to guess what you're gonna do with the rest of your money."

I'd saved sixty-five cents, and cones were only five cents each. The other two quarters were for something special. "That's for me to know and for you to find out!" I shouted, and punched him on the shoulder. Then I jumped up. "C'mon!" I ran into the hardware store, and Robert and Baby followed.

t w o

THE HIRAM HARDWARE STORE was stacked to the ceiling with tall dusty boxes full of knobs and brackets and metal hinges. I'm twelve now, but when I was little, I thought that if I pulled out one of those boxes all the way, there'd be a tiny square tunnel leading in from the world beyond our corner of Beulah County, Kentucky. I thought I might find secret messages there. Or, if I leaned in close, I might hear tales of wonder starring me, Jessica Kay Bovey. I knew there must be a bigger world that I was part of, only I was too little then to pull out any of those heavy boxes.

Finding your place in the world isn't that easy. Sometimes you have to push out and clear a space you can claim for yourself. And sometimes, when you're not even thinking about it, a space just opens up and you walk in and meet the outside world that's come looking for you. That's what happened to me when we ran into the Hiram Hardware store that day.

A woman I didn't know was standing in front of the counter. She was short and had gray hair. She was so plump

4

and neat, I thought she looked kind of like a fresh marsh-mallow with a brown belt around the middle. She turned and smiled at us as we came barging through the door.

Old Joe and Adam were waiting on her and Leroy Weaver. Adam was weighing out nails for Mr. Weaver while the stranger looked about, smiled, nodded, and answered one rapid-fire question after another from Adam's Uncle Joe.

"Yes, I'm staying with Mr. Weaver and his family up in Rockcastle," she answered. Rockcastle is one of the hollers around here.

"Not sure how long I'll be staying.

"Oh, yes, everybody's treating me fine.

"We'll be holding some meetings soon to find out what people around here need.

"I'll be working with the families in the hollows first."

I wasn't sure we could get a word in slantwise, but finally Adam got his uncle to quit giving her the third degree. Then Adam turned to us. "Well, right here, Miss Woodruff, you've got three of the finest, upstandingest citizens in Beulah County," he said.

"Hello. I'm Robert E. Ketchum," Robert said, and stepped right up to her with his hand stretched out. Robert has perfect manners, though God knows where he got them from since his daddy, Doyle, doesn't have a lick, and his mama, Beryl Ann, is usually working too hard to be around much. I figured he must have got them from all the books he's always reading.

"It's nice to meet you," said Miss Woodruff, taking Robert's hand and shaking it. "What does the 'E' stand for?"

"Eisenhower."

"Were you named after President Eisenhower?" she asked.

"Well, actually, no. After Robert E. Lee," Robert said. "But I just got the 'E' as a middle initial, and I'm still looking for the right name to go with it. So it could change."

"How interesting." Miss Woodruff beamed and turned to me. "And you are?"

I wiped my sticky hand on the seat of my jeans and held it out. "Jessie. Jessica K. Bovey. The 'K' just stands for Kay. That's K-a-y," I said, giving Robert a bug-eyed stare over Miss Woodruff's handshake.

"Nice to meet you," she replied. She looked at Baby. Sweat, dirt, and ice cream had caked into the rolls of fat around his neck and arms and, somehow, into his pale, almost white hair. His shorts were sliding off his round belly, and his thumb was in his mouth now that he was done with his ice cream. But he'd managed to keep his shoes on.

I pulled his thumb, with a little popping sound, from his mouth. "This is Baby Blue," I said. "He's four, but he doesn't talk much. He's Robert's brother."

Miss Woodruff held out her hand and solemnly shook Baby Blue's small, sticky one. "Another wonderful name," she commented.

"It's really Morton Ketchum. Their daddy, Doyle, named him after a box of salt. But he doesn't answer to that. We all call him Baby Blue because that's what their mama, Beryl Ann, calls him."

"I see."

Well, I wasn't about to tell a perfect stranger the whole story of how Doyle was so drunk the night Baby was born that all he could concentrate on was a box of salt in the hospital cafeteria.

We just stood there smiling at each other until Adam said, "You know, Miss Woodruff, Jessie lives in Baylor. She would be the perfect guide for you around there."

"Guide?" I said.

"I'm a VISTA volunteer," Miss Woodruff said. "It stands for Volunteers in Service to America. I'll be helping people get their medical problems attended to, finding out what kinds of educational needs people have, food and clothing, that sort of thing.

"And," she continued, smiling at us and nodding in Adam's direction, "I thought it'd be altogether nicer if someone local could introduce me. From talking to Mr. Weaver and these gentlemen, I get the impression people are leery of strangers coming up to their front door."

Joe said, "Leroy's oldest ones are helping in the fields right now, so we have to find somebody else who can show her around."

"Well, if *anybody* knows folks and their business," Adam put in, winking at me from under the John Deere baseball cap he always wore, "it's Jessie. I don't think her mother will mind. Mirabelle's pretty nice. And on a good day, with the wind in the right direction, Jessie's not liable to bite your head off, either." Even though Adam was about Mama's age, or a little older, he was always teasing us kids.

I started to fold my arms and give him my *Oh, yeah?* look

when Miss Woodruff asked, "Would you help me out? At least around Baylor?"

Miss Woodruff had an awfully friendly face. Her eyes had about a hundred laugh lines spiking out from behind her small round glasses. And I knew that Adam was a good judge of both people and dogs, even if he did like to pull my leg. "That'll be fine," I said, nodding at Miss Woodruff. "I'm sure Mama won't mind. There aren't that many people who live in Baylor anyway."

By this time Mr. Weaver was ready to head out with his purchases. So I told Miss Woodruff how to find my house and we all waved "bye now" to them.

After they'd left, Robert and I looked at each other with our eyebrows raised. "Staying with the Weavers?" we whispered, almost at the same time.

I wondered how they were putting her up, and I knew Robert was wondering the same thing. Mr. and Mrs. Weaver had so many kids that every bed in that old run-down house of theirs had at least three or four people sleeping in it. And I knew for a fact that their oldest boy, Ben, sometimes slept out in the barn. Surely they weren't making a grown woman sleep on a pallet on the floor?

The Weavers were about the poorest family in Beulah County. And even though this was 1967, and there was talk of going to the moon some day, the Weavers still didn't have running water. They had an outhouse out past their barn.

"Staying with the Weavers?" I asked Joe and Adam, louder. "Why?"

"Why?" Joe echoed. "Good question. I guess Leroy gets

some extra money for putting her up. She's one of those do-gooders from up North."

"She doesn't talk much like a Yankee," Robert said.

"Nope. She's originally from Cincinnati. But that's still north of the river."

"How does a VISTA person do all that stuff she talked about?" I asked.

"Another good question," said Joe, leaning on the countertop. "I think the way it works is that these volunteers come into a community and live with ordinary folks to find out what kinds of things we need. Then they go about helping us figure out how to get those things, or making arrangements to get the government to provide them. It's all part of some fancy plan President Johnson's got. A 'War on Poverty,' they're calling it."

"Poverty's a good thing to have a war against," Robert said.

"Sure it is," Joe replied. "The problem is, some people don't think they need any help, and the only thing up-North do-gooders do is get them all riled up. If she's not careful, it could be like stirring up a mess of red ants, especially since the mine over on Greasy Ridge closed and a lot of the miners are out of work."

"But helping someone's a good thing, isn't it?" I asked.

"Most times it is," Adam cut in. "Now, talking about helping"—he straightened up and looked professional—"how can we help you young people today?"

Robert and Baby both looked at me curiously. I'd almost forgotten. "I want to buy one of those raffle tickets the

Hiram Rotary's got for sale there," I said, and pointed to the sign on a red box on the counter.

Adam turned the box around and looked at the sign. "Well, we got us a problem. You have to be eighteen to purchase a raffle ticket in Beulah County. You see, it says so right there in little print. What were you going to do if you won those auto parts? Does your mama's car need fixing?"

I rocked back and forth a little bit before answering. "I was kind of hoping to get that second prize."

"I see," said Adam. "But you know, Jessie, even if you did win the dinner-for-two prize, you can't go to the Roadside Grill. They've got a bar and a floor show; they don't allow children in there."

"I know. I was just gonna let..." I didn't want to blurt this part out, but it looked like I was going to have to. "I was just gonna let my mama take...take whoever she wanted," I said, picking at a staple somebody had stapled into the edge of the counter. "Just...somebody." I shrugged.

I'd been planning this for ages, ever since I first heard about the raffle. I just *had* to get a ticket for Mama. She really needed to get out. Lately, she'd had to work more hours than ever at the Gas & Go because Lester was sick so much. I could see how tired she was.

I looked at Adam, leaning back, so tall against the shelves behind him, a curious smile on his tanned face, waiting for me to finish.

"OK, a date," I admitted, putting my hands on my hips and staring him dead in the eye.

Adam and Joe chuckled. They looked at each other, and

then over the counter at us. Adam cleared his throat and pushed back his baseball cap. "I see," he said. "Any idea *who* she might want to take?"

Now, if it had been anybody else besides my friends Joe and Adam laughing, I would have said it wasn't their business. Instead, I smiled at Adam and answered sweetly, "Not yet."

"Hmm," he replied. "In that case, how about I buy a ticket and promise to give you the prize if I win? I haven't bought one yet, and I was of a mind to do that very thing today. I don't know of any law that says I can't give away something I win, and I can't think of a better use to put it to if we *do* win."

"Great!" I said, and watched as Adam filled out a little slip of paper and put it in the Rotary box. Then I asked, "Can you buy another one? For Beryl Ann?"

Robert elbowed me—hard—in the side. I knew it was rude and all to ask for a double favor like that, but I wanted Beryl Ann, who was my mama's best friend and like a second mama to me, to have a chance to win, too. I stood my ground and never even glanced at Robert. Adam scratched his cheek for a moment.

"You can see I got fifty cents to pay you back with," I added, pulling my quarters out of my pocket. "That's enough for two chances. I earned it filling in for Mama and Lester at the Gas and Go."

"Sure, why not," said Adam, laughing.

"Thank you kindly," Robert said as Adam added another slip to the raffle box.

I gave Adam my fifty cents to pay for the drawing slips.

Then Robert and I each grabbed one of Baby's hands and left the store.

Just as we stepped out, we almost ran headlong into Dickie Whitten, who was riding past on his bike. Dickie lived between Baylor and Hiram, in Dog Gap Holler, and had just finished seventh grade, a year ahead of us.

"Watch it, Spaz Boy!" he yelled, swerving to keep from running into Robert on the sidewalk.

Now, there's a lot of stupid stuff I can take, but Dickie Whitten calling Robert Spaz Boy is not included. The way I see it, a person shouldn't go around making fun of other people about things they can't help, like Robert wearing glasses so thick he looked like he was always peeking out through a fishbowl. Last spring I'd punched Dickie and got sent home for it. But I didn't care, because Dickie had to come to school the next day with a black eye and all the kids knew I'd done it.

I let go of Baby's hand, pushed Dickie off his bike, and lit into him, fists flying. I didn't care if he was a boy and bigger than me. I didn't stop to think about that, or what was going to happen if I got caught fighting again. I just saw red all over, and Dickie Whitten's mean face right there in the middle of it.

three

"WHOA, GIRL. WHOA. STOP! Stop. It's OK now. Shh, OK. It's me—Adam." I could hear the voice, but the words didn't seem to have any connection to me, to right then, to my wanting to smash Dickie Whitten completely to smithereens.

It took me a while to realize that Robert must have gone back into the store and gotten Adam. And now my fists were swinging uselessly through the air as Adam hauled me off Dickie and held me up off the ground.

"What're you trying to do, Jessie? Whup your way into *The Guinness Book of World Records*?" Adam asked. "What is this, the third, fourth fight already? Summer's not even halfway over."

"It's just Dickie and his bigmouth friends!" I shouted as Dickie got up from the ground and wiped at his split lip. I'd landed a good one.

"You're crazy, you know that?" he yelled, leaning down and yanking his bike up from the sidewalk. "You and that four-eyed ree-tard that doesn't even know his own name, and his weird little brother. You're all crazy."

"Oh, I'll get you for that!" I screamed as I struggled to kick him.

"Dick, you'd do better to watch that mouth of yours," warned Adam.

"Yeah, says who?" Dickie snarled, spitting some blood. He jumped on his bike and took off. He was halfway down the block, jerkily pumping back and forth, when he yelled back over his shoulder, "At least I know who my daddy is!"

"Let me go," I ordered Adam, still struggling. "Let me go!"

"Whoa. Enough. You're not going anywhere," Adam said. He lowered me to the ground, keeping a firm hand on my shoulder.

"But, but...Robert is *not* retarded. He's the smartest kid I know." I had to make Adam understand. "Besides, Dickie Whitten deserves it. You heard what he just said." I gulped, yanked up on my jeans, and folded my arms. "So there."

Adam took off his baseball cap and brushed back his sandy-colored hair. He looked up at the sky and then down at me. "Jessie, Dickie may really rile you up good, but you've got to stop using your fists to make a point. There are better ways to deal with no-accounts like Dickie."

"Yeah. Well, right now, I can't think of a better one than punching his lights out," I said.

I stared off down the street, where Dickie had gone, riding straight out of Hiram, and then over at Robert and Baby Blue, who were coming back out of the store. Adam motioned for them to stay put. He put his cap back on and leaned against Mr. Appleby's old Ford truck. He gazed at my dirty clothes, at my scraped and bleeding elbows.

"Well," he said. He found a toothpick in his shirt pocket, put it in his mouth, and swiveled it around for a few moments. "Mirabelle's not going to be happy about this."

I looked down and kicked up a little gravel by the curb with the toe of my sneaker. Adam was right. Mama would probably ground me until I was thirty. But it sure had felt good to land one on Dickie's smirking face. "Robert's my best friend," I said. "And he does too know his own name."

Last year Robert had used Einstein as a middle name. Some of the kids, especially the older ones, had thought that was pretty dumb, and Dickie and some of his friends were still making fun of him. "He just likes to try on names and see how they fit, that's all."

I didn't want to talk about that other thing Dickie had shouted over his shoulder. Somewhere deep inside I was fighting back a sob. But I'd've died rather than have someone see me cry, even Adam. Especially here on Main Street with God-knows-who-all peeking out their windows. "Robert's not a spaz," I said. I concentrated on the toe of my sneaker. "And he can't help it if he's got to wear those glasses."

"I know that," Adam drawled. "But punching Dickie isn't going to stop him from saying mean things. Some folks are just plain mean, and nothing will stop them from being mean. They're mean until the day they die."

"Well, then, I wish he *would* die!"

"Now, now." Adam took the toothpick out of his mouth and pointed it at me. "What you have to do is find a way to keep yourself from getting so heated up—not to let what others say get to you. Besides"—he smiled—"you're almost

15

a pretty young lady now, almost as pretty as your mama, I think...somewhere—under all those scabs. You can't keep rolling around with boys in the dirt. Folks might get the wrong idea."

Had Adam gone round the bend? A pretty young lady? *Me?* And what was he thinking? That I *liked* to fight with boys? I squinted at him and said, slow-like, so he'd get my point real good, "You...are...as...crazy...as...Miss...Maybee's...old...dog...Cooch."

"Yeah." He laughed. Leaning away from the truck, he reached over and gave me a knuckle kiss on the top of my head. "Maybe I am. But you, young lady, have got to get control of yourself. And pretty quick, too, or you're going to be grounded until you're a senior citizen." Then we both laughed. He straightened up, took another look at me, and said, "Come on into the store. Let's see if we can clean you up a bit before Mirabelle sets eyes on you. Anyway, Uncle Joe owes me ten cents. He was betting on Dickie."

four

WE RODE BACK TO Baylor with Beryl Ann and her friend Lucy, who always dropped Beryl Ann off when they got done with their shifts at the Piggly Wiggly supermart in Hiram. Robert and I sat in the back seat with Baby between us.

"Why'd you have to go and do that?" he whispered.

"You heard him call you a spaz," I mouthed as quietly as I could so Beryl Ann wouldn't hear.

"You'll get in trouble again. Besides, everyone knows Dickie's an idiot."

"You can't let people push you around," I whispered back.

Robert leaned over Baby's head. "Dickie doesn't push me around. I just don't waste my time on him. I ignore him."

I leaned over Baby, too, so that Robert and I were practically nose-to-nose. "You'd ignore a Tyrannosaurus rex if it stepped on your foot!" I hissed.

"No, I wouldn't," Robert said. "Tyrannosaurus rexes are extinct. And if something extinct stepped on my foot, I'd..."

"I like dinosaurs," Baby said.

"Shh," I said. "We're not talking about dinosaurs."

"One *couldn't* step on Robert's foot, Jessie," Baby said, looking up at me. "They're dead."

Robert leaned back in the seat and laughed.

"What is it?" Beryl Ann asked, looking over her shoulder at us.

"It's nothing, Mama," Robert said. After Beryl Ann had turned back around, he shook his head and mouthed, "You're gonna get grounded."

"So? You think you know everything," I mouthed right back. And then we were at their house.

To get home, I just had to cross the road from the Ketchums' and cut across the vacant field where our old house used to stand. As I walked, I tried to figure out what I was going to say to Mama. I hoped I could get in and put on a long-sleeve shirt before she saw my scraped-up arms.

I swung the kitchen door open and peeked in. I didn't see Mama. But I'd only taken a step or two into the kitchen when she came round the corner with a basket of laundry and almost ran into me. She took one look at me and got that no-nonsense look on her face. "Jessica!"

"Yes'm?"

"Jessica, have you been fighting again?"

"Well." I cleared my throat. "I . . ." I looked at the floor and wondered if I could make Mama understand it this time.

"Jessica, we've had this talk a hundred times, it seems like. When are you going to stop fighting?"

"I know," I mumbled. I took a deep breath and plunged

in. "It was Dickie Whitten. He was picking on Robert again. And . . . and he said other stuff, too. I couldn't stand by and let him call Robert Spaz Boy, could I?"

Mama put the laundry basket down. "Robert has to fight his own fights his own way," she said. "Besides, you shouldn't stoop to Dickie's level. Just ignore his nonsense. Control yourself. You know we agreed that—"

"But it isn't fair!" I shouted, throwing my arms up in the air. I had to get Mama to see my side of it. "It isn't fair that Dickie can go around saying whatever in the world he wants to, even if it isn't true and even if it hurts people! And *I'm* the one who has to control myself?" I stamped my foot as hard as I could to make the tears stay back.

I guess Mama thought I was still hopping mad. "OK, young lady," she said, putting her hands on her hips, "to your room to cool down. And you're grounded for a week. No TV. No running over to visit with Lester or Robert."

Stomping down the hall, all I could think about was how sometimes life just isn't fair.

To make matters worse, it wasn't more than a half an hour later that Mama poked her head into my bedroom and told me that Grandma had stopped by and I was to come out and say hello. The only thing worse than being grounded was visiting with my grandmother.

"Is Chet with her?" I asked hopefully.

"No." Mama shook her head and whispered, "Grandma just finished up in court. They're divorced."

"Oh, no." I sighed. I'd liked this husband.

Grandma was often the talk of the neighborhood. Even

though she only lived a little ways away in Bartlettsville, the county seat, we never saw much of her while she was married. Unfortunately, she didn't stay married. She had up and divorced every one of my step-grandpas. And my real grandpa, Grandpa Henry, had died before I was born. Some folks wondered if she hadn't gotten rid of him, too.

It was too bad that she was divorced again. It meant she'd be coming around to keep an eye on us, as she liked to say. For some reason we needed "keeping an eye on" only when the Ol' Biddy was single.

I shuffled out of my bedroom.

five

GRANDMA AND I HAD always rubbed each other the wrong way. From as far back as I could remember, she had always complained about Mama letting me run wild like a "regular tomboy." She always hated every single pet I brought home. And the fact that everyone calls me "Jessie" drives her crazy. "What kind of a name is that for a girl!" Grandma complains. "It's a man's name," she says, and usually adds, "Jessica is a perfectly fine name."

When she caught sight of me, the first thing out of her mouth was, "Would you look at her, Mirabelle. She's a mess." No "Howdy, how ya doing?" Not even a hug. That's my grandma for you.

Grandma was always trying on new getups, and today was no exception. She'd dyed her hair again, and she reminded me of a white turnip with stiff red curls sprouting up on top. She had on a pair of pink stretch pants that clashed with her new color.

"Hi, Grandma," I said, slipping into a kitchen chair.

"What mud hole have you been wallowing in?" she asked.

"I'm too old to play in mud holes," I said.

"You can't tell that from the looks of you," Grandma said, and snorted like she was disgusted.

Well, it wasn't exactly smooth as gravy at our house right then, and it always went from bad to worse once the Ol' Biddy got revved up. Fortunately, Mama cut in, and I managed to weasel out of the kitchen after a few minutes of being lectured about "ladylike" behavior.

Back in my room, I tried to engage Mr. Perkins, my pet toad, in a conversation to drown out Mama's and Grandma's voices. But I had woken him up from a deep sleep and he wasn't going to keep up his end of things. I could barely get a few blinks out of him.

I knew Grandma would get around to her favorite topic sooner or later, and I just wasn't in the mood. It usually went like this: Even though I'd had the misfortune to be born "without the benefit of wedlock," I needed a father now, and what was Mama doing burying herself in a hick town like Baylor and working herself to death at a dead-end job at the Gas & Go?

When she really got rolling, I tried to block it all out by singing to Mr. Perkins. "Swing low, sweet chariot," I sang. But I heard little bits here and there—the usual thing. And all I was doing was putting Mr. Perkins back to sleep, so I stopped.

"Maybe if we'd gotten you married quickly," I heard Grandma say, "you'd be out of Baylor by now. Maybe you could have gone on and gotten your nursing degree, *been* somebody. Maybe you would have gotten to know some of the *nice* people at the hospital — besides that so-called doctor friend of yours."

"I *am* somebody, Mama. I'm happy here in Baylor," Mama said. "And how many times do I have to tell you — Warren really *is* a doctor."

Grandma was well into her favorite subject now. I opened my bedroom door a crack and leaned my forehead on the door frame, listening. I'd heard it about a thousand times before.

"Well," Grandma said, "I've never seen the likes. All I know is, you followed him around all the time when he was here. And has he ever *once* offered to help you get set up up North someplace?"

"Mother, I did *not* follow him around. Besides," added Mama, "I don't want to be set up up North. I'm set up just fine where I am. Maybe someday, when Lester's ready to sell the Gas and Go, I'll be able to buy it."

"That store!" Grandma yelped. "You can't seriously be thinking about chaining yourself to a run-down gas pump and a few grocery shelves for the rest of your life! When I was married to Martin, we went to Las Vegas. Now *there's* someplace I'd like to live, always something to do. You might like it there."

"I'm not interested in living in Las Vegas," Mama said. I could hear her getting up and putting dishes in the sink. She was probably looking out the window and across the road toward the Gas & Go right now.

"All right. Not Las Vegas, then. Even Bartlettsville is better than this excuse for a town. At least they've got a couple of decent stores and restaurants. Maybe you could meet people there, get out some, instead of hiding here."

There was a long pause. I knew Mama's patience was wearing thin. "I don't want to move," Mama said. "I like the people here, now. It isn't like it used to be. Besides, Lester's not well, and he needs me." I could just picture her shoulders slumping.

I figured it was about time for the cavalry to come to her rescue. I picked up Mr. Perkins and walked back into the kitchen, making lots of warning noises along the way.

Grandma was just saying, "Well, I've always been afraid that you'd end up here forever, since that old fool Lester let you live in this house. I know that after your daddy died — bless his soul — and that house of ours burned, I took the first chance I could to get out of here. You've got Jessica to think about, and she's starting to grow up."

"Hi, sweetie," Mama said as I came into the kitchen. She opened her arms so I could walk into them. I could tell right then that I'd made my appearance in the nick of time because she didn't seem to be mad at me anymore. I'm getting way too old to be babied, but it sure felt good to be standing there leaning against Mama with her arms clasped about my waist — me and Mama, together, smiling at the Ol' Biddy.

Grandma looked at Mr. Perkins. "That's exactly what I'm talking about. Is a frog any kind of a pet for a growing girl? Really, Jessica!" she snapped.

"Mr. Perkins is a toad," I said, holding him out to her, "and Robert told me it's a scientific fact that toads are smarter than frogs. But if you don't like Mr. Perkins, I think there're a couple of baby copperheads in a Mason jar around here, someplace. Baby Blue found them by the creek yesterday."

Grandma didn't even look at me. She just stood up and walked out, saying, "Lord, Mirabelle. What are you going to do with this little hellion?"

I shifted Mr. Perkins, raised my right hand, and slowly waved goodbye as the screen door slammed. Then we heard her brand-new pure white Thunderbird start up. One thing you can say about my grandma, she sure knows how to get a new car out of each husband before he hightails it.

"Jessie," Mama choked, turning me around. She shook her finger at me like she was trying to say something stern but wanted to laugh. Finally, she got her voice back and said, "You know Grandma's frightened to death of snakes."

Then she stopped shaking her head and brushed the hair out of my eyes. "You are the light of my life," she whispered. I waited for her to kiss me on my forehead before letting me go. "But you're still grounded, young lady. And you and your grandmother have to learn to get along one of these days. You know she only wants the best for us."

"The best for us is to stay here in Baylor."

"Oh, don't worry." Mama sighed. "We're not going anywhere. And *you* are staying here in this house this week, doing chores, while you think about how to control your temper and your tongue."

s i x

I TRUDGED BACK TO my room with Mr. Perkins. I thought about Grandma, my temper, and the fact that Dickie was right. I had no idea who my father was.

Mama wouldn't talk about it. When I was little, I used to ask her if I had a daddy like Robert and the other kids did. She always got really quiet and said of course I did and that someday, when the time was right, she'd tell me about him. I hadn't brought it up in ages because I'd begun to think the time was never going to be right, and it always seemed to make Mama sad.

But lately a lot of things were starting to pile up. And how was I supposed to learn to control my temper when no one would even talk to me about things that were important? It just wasn't fair.

I couldn't help getting mad at Dickie. That morning, before we'd walked to Hiram, I'd asked Robert when he was going to get his new glasses and he'd shrugged and looked away. Robert's gotten new glasses practically every summer that I could remember. I knew he needed them again because he brought his books up even closer to his face than usual in order to read. When I asked Baby later why Robert was still wearing his old glasses, Baby had said, "No money." How could he *not* get them this year?

I knew Beryl Ann and Doyle were poor. Beryl Ann didn't make much money at the Piggly Wiggly, and Doyle had stacks of hubcaps by their drive that he sold whenever he could. He had worked part-time at the mine, and now the mine was closed. Also, it didn't help that Doyle drank away half of their money at the Howling Kitty bar. Folks were always saying "How the mighty have fallen," what with Baylor being named after Doyle's own great-grandfather, Baylor Ketchum. I guess the Ketchums had a lick or two of horse sense back then.

It wasn't fair that Robert couldn't get his glasses. It wasn't fair that I had to control myself and Dickie Whitten could get away with being mean. It wasn't fair that I had a grandma who was an old biddy and that I'd never even met my real grandpa, Grandpa Henry, who'd died while Mama was still a girl. It wasn't fair that all I ever had was a bunch of step-grandpas who never hung around for very long, even when I liked one of them. It wasn't fair that I didn't have a father— at all. And it *really* wasn't fair, now that I was grounded for a week, that I wouldn't be able to go to the raffle drawing to see if I'd won a prize for Mama or Beryl Ann. None of it was fair.

I needed to talk to Lester. Lester always listened and talked to me straight, not like I was a baby. But even if I wasn't grounded, I probably wouldn't have been able to go over anyway, because Mama was worried about Lester's health.

Lester's about the oldest old person in Baylor—not that we have many people to begin with. Baylor's only got 128. Well, 127 if you don't count Old Wiley Whiteside, who's not supposed to, but does, live in the tire shack on this side of the Greasy Ridge Cemetery.

Anyway, Lester's pretty old, even older than Old Wiley. He says he was born in the last century, the 1800s. He lives right across the road from us, next to the Gas & Go, which is the only grocery or filling station between Bartlettsville and Hiram. Lester knows every mortal soul in Baylor and hereabouts.

He knows lots of other things, too, like how to tell one kind of toad call from another. Does anybody else know that there's more than one kind of toad call? Or more than one kind of toad? I didn't, not until Lester told me.

Lester lets me ring up customers on the cash register—if Mama's not working there to worry that I'm doing it right and the customers aren't the really cranky ones like Mrs. Beaumont. Also, he lets me help him in the garden and around his house. He tells me stories while we work, about when he was in Europe before the First World War and about all the "lookers" he liked to take out dancing. That always makes me laugh. I can't imagine Lester dancing, because he walks with a cane now. But he swears he was known far and wide for his fancy dancing steps.

I think Lester likes having kids around because he misses his own family. When you're Lester's age, a lot of folks have died on you already. His wife has been dead for years. And they'd only had but one child, Darlene. She and Grandma went to school together. Grandma said she thought Darlene was somewhere up North, maybe Detroit. But Lester hadn't heard from her in so many years he didn't know if she was still alive. And his only grandson, Jack, died in a car accident.

Anyway, I hadn't been over to visit Lester for a couple of days because Mama said he needed some peace and quiet. So Robert and I, and Baby, had stayed away. Now I'd have to wait a whole week to visit, and I'd have to think about all this by myself.

I stroked Mr. Perkins's back with my fingertip, the way he liked it, and stared out the window toward our vacant field and Martin's Mountain. Even if I couldn't visit Lester, there was at least one thing I could do. I'd get an answer to one big question I'd had for a long time, and maybe put an end to Dickie's mean remarks, too.

I put Mr. Perkins in his glass tank, got out some paper and a pencil, and wrote...

July 19, 1967

Dear Dr. Harrison,

My name is Jessie K. Bovey. You knew my mother, Mirabelle Bovey, and my grandmother, Anna Mae Bovey, when you were working in Hiram. Mama says you are a special friend of hers and talks about you a lot.

Anyway, in school when we were practicing communications, Mr. Prichard said to get right to the point in a business letter. So my point is, are you my father?

If you are, I would appreciate it very much if you could stop by for a visit and say "Hello." I have some things I'd like to talk to you about. Thank you for your time.

Sincerely,
Jessie K. Bovey

P.S. I'm a girl and was born on January 13, 1955.

I'd always had a sneaking suspicion about Mama's doctor friend. He was working in Hiram at the time I started to make my presence known. And there were some of his letters that Mama wouldn't let me read. Besides, Grandma always snorted or shook her head when his name was mentioned. So if Mama wasn't going to talk to me, well, I *was* twelve years old, and I reckoned that was plenty old enough to start taking matters into my own hands. Oh, boy, wouldn't Dickie swallow his tongue if he knew my daddy was a doctor!

I felt much better once I'd written the letter and looked it over. It was to the point but still friendly. Just the way Mr. Prichard, our sixth-grade teacher, said business letters should be.

Now I just had to find his address. I tiptoed down the hall and into the kitchen and peeked out the screen door. Mama must have finished hanging up the laundry after Grandma left and gone over to the store or to Lester's. The coast was clear. I went into her bedroom and rummaged through the top drawer of her desk. Her address book had gotten stuck in the back of the drawer, and when I pulled it out, I pulled out a crinkled letter, too. It was to Mama from...yes! There it was. Dr. Warren Harrison's return address in Chicago was on the envelope.

I snatched up a fresh envelope and a stamp from the top of the desk—I hoped Mama wouldn't notice just one missing. I smoothed out the crumpled-up envelope and copied the address. Then, before I stuffed the letter and address book back into Mama's drawer, I turned that envelope over and over in my hands. I wondered if this was one of his letters Mama hadn't let me read.

I ran my fingers over the neat, small writing of the address. Should I open it and read it? I glanced out Mama's bedroom window to make sure she wasn't on her way back. I turned the envelope over again. If he was my father, didn't I have a right to read it?

I bit my lip and looked at myself in the mirror. Finally, I realized that I'd been standing there for ages. At this rate, Mama was going to catch me. Quickly, I spread open the slit at the top and peeked in. I took a deep breath and glanced up at the window just in time to see Mama coming across the yard.

I shoved the letter and the address book into the back of the drawer, slammed it shut, and ran into my bedroom. I slipped my letter under the lining in my nightstand drawer and lay down on my bed to catch my breath. I was shaking a little. If Mama had caught me, she would have grounded me forever.

Somehow I'd sneak my letter out to Robert to mail while I was grounded, and then that would be one thing taken care of. Now all I had left to figure out was how to get a nicer grandmother, how to control my temper as I'd promised Mama over and over that I would, and how to help Robert get the new glasses he needed.

I must have fallen asleep, because the next thing I knew it was starting to get dark and Mama was sitting by my side, brushing my bangs back and kissing me on the forehead. "Wake up, light of my life," she whispered. I pretended to be sleeping to keep her there a bit longer. "Time for dinner. Even if you are grounded, you still have to eat."

"Hmm," I mumbled and slowly opened my eyes to look at her. Adam was right; I do have a pretty mama. Her hair is dark and wavy, and when she lets it down, it hangs just below her shoulders. Most of the time she wears it up in a ponytail to keep it out of her way. I think that makes her look even younger than most of the other mothers around, even Mrs. Salyer, Missy's tiny little mama. And she's got a lot of freckles, like me. The big difference between us is that Mama's got soft brown eyes and mine are plain old green. People say I don't have her smile, either.

I thought about that sometimes and wondered who else had my green eyes. Grandma didn't. She had brown eyes, like Mama's. Maybe Grandpa Henry did. I didn't even know that. And whose smile *did* I have?

I raised my hand up and touched Mama's sleeve. "I'm not very hungry."

"It's your favorite, bean soup," Mama said, kissing the back of my hand.

I said, "I've been thinking about not fighting, like you told me to. Only it's hard not to when someone like Dickie is being mean and saying hurtful things."

"I know it is, sweetie," Mama said. "But that's when you need to be really strong. Look at Robert. He doesn't let it get to him."

"I know. I wish I could be more like Robert, Mama, but I don't know how. I just get so mad, especially if Dickie calls Robert or Baby Blue a name. It's not right."

"Jessie, you've been trying to protect Robert since the two of you were in diapers and shared the same playpen. I know he's like a brother to you, and it's good to stick up for your friends. But Robert does a good job of taking care of himself. You need to quit worrying about what others say when they're being mean," Mama said. "Just stick your nose up in the air and show them you couldn't care less. When you give in and fight, they know they've gotten under your skin.

"Besides, defending Robert and Baby doesn't explain the other times you've let your temper get the best of you. What about Missy and the spiders you pinned on her mother's pomander ball in Girl Scouts? That didn't have anything to do with Robert or Baby Blue, now, did it?"

I leaned way up on my elbows toward her. "Oh, that." I hesitated, kind of wishing Mama hadn't brought up the fact that I'd been asked not to come back to Girl Scouts after causing a little ruckus at Missy's house last year. How was I to know that Mrs. Salyer was scared of spiders? "That Missy Salyer was getting to me with all her 'My daddy this' and 'My daddy that,'" I said. "Besides, who the heck needs a pomander ball with little cloves stuck all over it to stink up your clothes anyway?"

"Jessica," Mama said.

"Oh, all right. Missy's OK, I guess. Sometimes I like her. But I didn't want to hear any more about her daddy's car dealerships and where they stayed at Disneyland. I bet my daddy is richer and nicer than hers any ol' day."

Mama sat back fast and it took me a minute to realize what I'd said and why this strange, sad look had suddenly come on her face. "Mama? I'm sorry, Mama. It just came out without thinking."

She was staring off into space.

"It's OK, Mama!" I sat up and grabbed her around the waist. "I didn't mean anything by that. Honest. I've just got a bad temper, that's all. And sometimes I say stuff I don't really mean. I'll try harder. I promise." I threw my arms around her, and the sob that had been hiding inside me all day escaped. I hid my face in Mama's blouse and cried.

seven

THE NEXT MORNING I think Mama was surprised to find Miss Woodruff at our door. What with Grandma's visit and being grounded and all, I'd completely forgotten to tell Mama she was coming.

Mama invited her in, and they talked for a long time in the kitchen about the volunteer work Miss Woodruff was doing. Then Mama let me have a reprieve to go with Miss Woodruff.

"I hope you don't mind helping me out," Miss Woodruff said as we walked up our drive toward the road.

"No, ma'am!" I told her, taking a few high skips. "It's fine. I was gonna be stuck inside, and now I get to show you around instead. Only there aren't that many folks that live in Baylor. Leastways, ones whose houses you can get to easily.

"Well, let's see," I said, stopping at the end of the drive. "Which way do you want to go first?"

We looked up the one patched-over paved road that runs through Baylor and climbs up the skinny valley from the iron bridge at the Little Red River. Past the Ketchum place the road divides, with one branch headed toward Hiram and the other to Bartlettsville. Baylor also has some two-lane dirt tracks that wander up the mountainsides and into the hollers where a good number of folks farm corn or run cattle in steep-sided pastures.

"Let's do what we can on foot here in the downtown first," said Miss Woodruff. "Then, if there's time, or on another day, I'll take my car and we can drive up in the hollows. I'd like to get to Greasy Ridge or through Dog Gap and visit the families there soon."

I smiled. I'd never heard anyone say that Baylor had a "downtown" before. I wasn't sure if one combined gas station–grocery store–post office, one church, and fifteen houses equaled a downtown or not.

I turned left and started toward the river. Thinking about the families up in the hollers, I asked, "How're the Weavers treating you?"

"Just fine," Miss Woodruff said. "It is very kind of them to put me up."

"They aren't making you sleep on a pallet, are they?"

"No." Miss Woodruff smiled. "I'm sharing a bed with Vergie, the oldest girl, and with Joycelin. She's about eight." She laughed. "I think sometimes their baby brother crawls in, too. It's cozy, but I don't mind. Staying there gives me some ideas about what the people here need."

As we walked, I pointed out the Beaumont house, the Clawson place, Mr. Dutton's, and Miss Doolittle's. We stopped at all of them, but only Mrs. Clawson and Mr. Dutton were home. They nodded politely when I introduced Miss

Woodruff. When I told them that her job was to see what kinds of things she and the government could help us with, Mr. Dutton said that the church needed a new coffeepot. He said the old one had gotten queerly rewired, and when it percolated, it was way too dramatic for his druthers. Miss Woodruff laughed out loud at that. She allowed she knew what he meant, and said she'd think about how she could help the church get a new one.

Beyond the river the mountains rise up steeply and the road snakes off toward Greasy Creek. So we stayed on the Baylor side of the river and crossed the road at the bridge to start back up toward the church and the Gas & Go. We stopped at the Smiths', at Boot Milton's, and at Mrs. Boyd's house. They, and everybody else, were really polite to Miss Woodruff, and she made a point of shaking everybody's hand.

"That," I said, pointing up ahead, "is the New Revivalist Baptist Mission Church. Preacher Beaumont isn't too bad to listen to. Every so often he gets the call and herds everybody down to the river to get rebaptized—'revived,' he calls it— in its waters. It's kind of fun to watch the congregation come out all soaking wet."

Miss Woodruff laughed again. I liked that about her. And there was something about her I knew I could trust. "I'm not much of a churchgoer," I confided.

"Why not?" she asked.

"Well, it's not that I don't believe in God and the Bible and all. I do. It's just that Mrs. Beaumont—she's Preacher's wife—says I'll probably burn in hellfire anyway."

"Oh, my!" gasped Miss Woodruff, stopping in her tracks to turn and stare at me. "Now, why in the world would she say such a thing to a child?"

"She says that bast— You see," I leaned in toward her and explained, "I haven't got a daddy. So Mrs. Beaumont, she says kids like me—that don't have fathers—are abominations anyhow."

Miss Woodruff straightened up and sucked in her cheeks so hard I thought she might turn herself inside out. Then she pushed up her glasses. "That's ridiculous!" she sputtered. "I've never...never heard such nonsense in my entire life."

"Yeah, well." I shrugged my shoulders and took off up the road again, leaving Miss Woodruff to compose herself and catch up.

"So I don't go to church much," I continued a few moments later. "Besides, they're always going on about repenting your sins and stuff. I figure I'm not old enough to have too many yet—except, of course, that one big one, getting born. But I didn't have a say about that, you know? I mean, if I could, I'd go out and get a daddy tomorrow. It just ain't an easy thing to do."

I thought about my letter to Dr. Harrison. "Anyway, I'm kind of working on that. And I'm saving up on my sins and figure I'll do my repenting all at once and get it over with. That way I only have to get my clothes wet once. I don't plan on doing much sinning after that."

We came to the Gas & Go and stopped in. I introduced Miss Woodruff to Lester, who was back at work for a bit. I watched the counter and ran the register while they talked about the president's War on Poverty and VISTA volunteers. Lester seemed really pleased, and the two of them chatted for a good long time.

I didn't get much of a chance to speak with Lester myself other than to tell him I was grounded again. He shook his head and squeezed my hand as Miss Woodruff and I left. Sometimes Lester and I understand each other without having to use a lot of words.

Lester's house was right next door to the Gas & Go. I'd just pointed it out to Miss Woodruff when Baby Blue came out the front door with a slice of white bread in each hand.

"Did you put the rest of Lester's bread away after you got some?" I asked. Baby nodded at me and fell into step with us. "Where's Robert?" I asked.

"Don't know," Baby said. He shrugged and bit into his bread. Robert was probably out looking for him right now.

"We're headed up your way," I said. "We'll walk you home."

"Does Lester have other family living at home?" Miss Woodruff asked.

"No. Lester lives all by himself."

Miss Woodruff gave me a funny look. "Baby Blue just came out...." Her voice trailed off and she pointed at Lester's house.

It took me a second to figure out what Miss Woodruff was getting at. Then I understood. "Oh. It's OK," I said to her. "When he's hungry, Baby Blue just goes in wherever he's at and helps himself."

"You mean, he goes into other people's houses when they're not home?"

"Yup." I nodded. "People don't mind. Everybody knows there's a good chance that Baby will come through while they're at work or somewhere. Some folks even leave stuff out for him—except Preacher's wife. She locks her door."

"Doesn't he get enough to eat at home?"

"Sure! Beryl Ann's a good cook. It's just that Baby doesn't want to go all the way back home if he's hungry. Old Mr. Dutton says Baby 'goes grazing.' I think people's houses are just like the woods and the river and the mountains round here to Baby—some place to wander through and graze in. That's all."

"I see," Miss Woodruff answered thoughtfully. "He doesn't...I mean, he doesn't...?"

"Oh, Baby would never steal anything or tear anything up, if you're wondering about that," I offered. "He mostly just eats, though he might move something from one place to another after studying on it.

"Take Lester's Bible, for example. Lester used to grumble, because every time Baby passed through his house looking for something to eat he'd move the Bible from the reading table to the little table by the back door. And after every one of Baby's visits, Lester would have to move it back. Finally, Lester gave in and left it by the back door. Now every time Lester goes in or out of the house, he puts his hand on the Good Book. And you know what?" I asked Miss Woodruff.

"What?"

"Lester says it feels right natural, like the Lord is watching over all his comings and goings, and he wouldn't have his Bible anywhere else but there by the back door. You see what I mean? I think Baby Blue's got a feel for how things ought to be."

"Hmm." She nodded as if she understood, and we both watched Baby munch on the second slice.

We had worked our way through the "downtown" section of Baylor by now and had stopped in front of the long drive up to the Ketchums' house. I didn't see Doyle's truck, and I knew Beryl Ann was at work. She always went in early.

"Looks like you'll have to come back later to meet Beryl Ann," I said.

"What about *Mr.* Ketchum?" asked Miss Woodruff.

I sure wasn't going to tell her that she could probably find him at the Howling Kitty. I said, "Sometimes he's around. But I wouldn't count on catching him."

"OK." She nodded. "I'll try to meet Mrs. Ketchum later."

We waited while Baby finished the last of the bread. Then Robert came around from the back of the house.

"Go on," I said to Baby, and gave him a little push up their steep drive. "Robert's probably worried about you."

I waved to Robert, but he didn't wave back.

eight

THE NEXT PLACE WAS up the road a piece, the Stanley farm, near Dog Gap Holler. So we decided to cross the road in front of the Ketchums' and stop at Miss Maybee's and then finish up back at my house. Miss Maybee's house was next to the field where our old house used to stand before it burned down.

We walked partway up the dirt drive and stopped. Miss Maybee's old dog, Cooch, was standing on his head in the yard.

"That's Cooch," I said. "Isn't he great?"

"My goodness!" Miss Woodruff said. "What in the world is he doing?"

"Just standing on his head. He does it a couple of times a day."

"But...how?"

I could tell Miss Woodruff, as she stood there with her mouth open, was plumb amazed. "He runs around in about twenty zillion circles first," I told her. "Then he props his head on a rock or clump of grass and hikes his bottom up.

He's so short, I think his hind feet just naturally come up off the ground.

"Miss Maybee thinks he does it only when he smells a critter like a chipmunk or a ground squirrel. She says he just wants to rub his head on the ground where there's a good smell. But Robert and I swear he does it because he likes to. We're going to time him one day and see how long he can stay up."

"What kind of dog is he?" Miss Woodruff asked.

"Just an old mixed-mutt hound. Nobody knows for sure," I said. "But he's pretty famous around here."

"I bet!" Miss Woodruff laughed.

"Be careful when you talk to Miss Maybee," I warned. "We all say Cooch is crazier than a junebug on a string, but she doesn't like to hear that."

"I'll keep that in mind," she said as we passed Cooch and went to the front porch.

Like most of the other folks in town, Miss Maybee was glad to make Miss Woodruff's acquaintance even though she didn't have any ideas about what Baylor might need from President Johnson. But she promised to think about it.

When Miss Woodruff was through talking with Miss Maybee, we headed out. Cooch was still on his head.

"Do you think that's harmful to him?" Miss Woodruff wondered aloud.

I shrugged my shoulders. "I don't think so, or he wouldn't keep doing it, would he? Robert is always going on about how we should enter him in *The Guinness Book of World Records*. He's studying up on how we go about doing that."

Just past Miss Maybee's was the corner of our property. I led the way along the path through the waist-high grass in our vacant field. "You aren't afraid of snakes, are you?" I asked.

"No. Why?" asked Miss Woodruff, suddenly stopping.

"It's OK," I said. "Just asking. My grandma's deathly afraid of them. She won't take the path; afraid they'll crawl out of the weeds at her. She drives everywhere. But I've only seen a few along here, mostly old black snakes. And I've only seen one copperhead here. They're mostly over along the loose rocks at the back," I said, waving toward the rear of the property where Martin's Creek zigzagged down to the river.

"Oh."

"Don't worry. I've been up and down this path barefoot all my life, and I can spot a snake at ten yards. I've never seen a rattlesnake in here. Lester killed a big one over at the Gas and Go, though, a couple of years ago. It was out sunning itself, right on the concrete there. It pretty near gave Mrs. Boyd a fit."

"Oh, dear," Miss Woodruff said.

I hummed a little as we walked single file through the tall weeds. I thought about how nobody had given Miss Woodruff any really good ideas on how the War on Poverty could help folks. The only person who said we needed something was Mr. Dutton. And that was just a coffeepot. "Miss Woodruff," I asked over my shoulder, "do you think you can get a new coffeepot for the church?"

She laughed. "Oh, I think we can come up with some way of doing that. I'm here to help out, however I can."

I thought about what she'd said all the way back to my house. When we got there, I sat down on the porch step and picked at the little white label on my sneaker. Miss Woodruff sat down, too.

"Miss Woodruff, I've been thinking," I said. "You said the War on Poverty is about trying to help poor people."

"That's right."

"Well, Beryl Ann and Doyle are poor, and Robert needs a new pair of glasses. Just a few minutes ago he didn't even see me wave at him when we dropped Baby off. His eyes are really bad."

Miss Woodruff nodded. "I noticed that," she said.

"He usually gets new glasses every summer. But this year he hasn't yet."

"Why not?"

"Baby says it's because they don't have the money. I figure that's on account of their daddy being laid off with the mine closing. Robert won't talk about it. But he needs them before school starts again."

I glanced over at Miss Woodruff. "So I was wondering, if you think you can get a new coffeepot for the church, do you think you could also get Robert some new glasses?"

Miss Woodruff crossed her legs and tapped her chin. "We might be able to help...a little. Glasses like the ones Robert needs are fairly expensive, I would think."

"How much do you figure a pair would cost?" I asked.

"At least thirty or forty dollars. Maybe more."

"That's a lot."

"Well, in needy situations the government will pay for

45

some dental and medical help for children. There's a special program for young children — an early school we call Head Start. I just don't know about eyeglasses, though, and Robert's too old for the Head Start program. It's for kids before they go to kindergarten. I'd have to check into it. One thing's for certain," she said. "The government won't pay the whole bill."

Miss Woodruff was quiet for a moment and then continued. "If Beryl Ann can come up with, oh, say, twenty dollars or so, maybe I can get the rest covered as a special need. But I can't promise you anything, Jessie."

"Twenty dollars. That's still a lot of money, especially for the Ketchums." I sighed. "Thank you," I said. I didn't want Miss Woodruff to think I was ungrateful.

"I'll see what I can do, Jessie. Why don't you talk to Mrs. Ketchum? Maybe there's some way you and Robert can help raise the money if it's more than she can get together right now. Where does Robert go to get his glasses?"

"Bartlettsville. There's a special eye doctor there, but I don't know his name."

"That's OK, I'll figure that bit out," she said and jumped up, brushing the dust off the back of her dress. She leaned toward me and tilted my chin up. "Think of it as a challenge. And I bet anything you're one for taking on a challenge and seeing it through to the end."

Then she straightened up and thanked me for taking her around the neighborhood. I waved goodbye and smiled as I watched her get into her car and drive off.

Now, somehow, we needed to get twenty dollars. That

wasn't going to be easy. I knew twenty dollars was about half of what Mama made in a week working at the Gas & Go.

And I knew I wasn't going to talk to Beryl Ann about it, or even Robert. Deep down I was afraid it'd be like that bike for Robert that Beryl Ann was always saving up for. I mean, you can save and save and save, but if all you can afford is a tiny bit out of a tiny bit, you just keep saving forever. It'd be next year, or longer, before Robert got new glasses. Already he took so much teasing. It'd only be worse if he started school this year hardly able to see. No. He needed them *now*, and I had to help.

nine

I KNEW THE REST of the week was going to drag by as slow as pouring molasses in January. But the next morning I got up early, determined to do everything Mama wanted done and to do it right.

I didn't have to worry about staying busy. Mama had lined up what seemed like a whole year's worth of chores. She had me cleaning out closets, scrubbing the bathroom — even dusting on top of the picture frames and the doors, which everyone knows nobody except a giant could ever see.

While I worked, I thought about the letter I'd written and hidden in the secret place in my nightstand drawer. I wondered what Dr. Warren Harrison was doing right now. Maybe he was delivering a baby, or doing brain surgery. Maybe he'd come for a visit and invite me to go back to Chicago and tour his hospital. Maybe he would want to work at the Hiram hospital again. Why not? He could work here and be the biggest doctor in the hospital. Boy, wouldn't Grandma snort about him then! I was smiling as I started to sweep the kitchen floor.

When I went to sweep the dirt out the door, I found

Robert sitting on our porch step, staring out at the field. Sometimes he does that—he just shows up.

"Hey!" I said.

He turned and said, "I told you you'd get grounded."

Honestly! Robert was getting almost as bad as Grandma about not saying howdy. "So?" I shrugged, and bit my tongue. Even though he's such a goody two-shoes sometimes, I didn't want to get in an argument with him today. I was glad to see him.

Besides, he'd been right. "OK," I said, giving in. "I guess I didn't really need to slug Dickie, even if he did deserve it. But listen," I rushed on, "can you do me a favor?"

"What?"

"Just a second and I'll tell you."

I ran into my room and got the letter. "Will you take this and mail it?" I opened the door and thrust it at him.

"Why don't you just give it to your mama to mail?" he asked.

"Because . . . because it's a surprise."

"Oh, no. The last time you surprised somebody, Mrs. Salyers fainted and almost had to be taken to the hospital," he said.

"It wasn't that bad. Besides, how was I to know she was scared of spiders? Nobody's going to faint over this." Or at least I hoped not. "C'mon, Robert, will you just do this one small thing for me? Please?"

"I'm always doing stuff for you," he said. "I did half your homework this year so you could pass sixth grade."

"No, you didn't!"

Robert tilted his head and stared at me.

"Oh, all right. Maybe you did," I said. But he'd *always* helped me with my homework since we were real little. He liked schoolwork. "Anyway, can you do this, please?" I asked again.

Robert sighed. He took the letter and held it up close to his face. "It's to a doctor.... I don't know about this."

"It's a good surprise, believe me. I've been working on it for a while."

After I assured him about twenty times that he wouldn't be an accessory to anything bad, I talked him into running the letter over to the Gas & Go and sneaking it into the mailbox by the door when Mama wasn't looking. I knew I could depend on Robert.

I flipped back the living-room curtains to peek out as he looked in the store window, walked over to the mailbox, and slid the letter into the slot. *Good! That's done,* I said to myself as I watched Robert walking home.

I was going to get started on my next chore when I passed Mama's bedroom door. I thought about the letter from Dr. Harrison I'd found in her drawer. Had it gotten stuck there, or was she hiding it? I knew it wasn't right, but I wondered if I ought to peek at that letter. Maybe he'd written something about me in it?

Mama would be working all afternoon and I wouldn't have to worry about getting caught this time. I went into her room and opened the desk drawer. I reached in and rooted around, but the letter wasn't there. Even her address book was gone. I bent down and looked way back. Nothing there but pencils and chewing gum and some odd scraps of paper. That was strange. I stood up and looked through the stuff on the top of her desk. There was the address book, under the telephone book. Mama must have gotten it out and used it. Ah! There was the letter, too.

I held it lightly in my hand and sat on the edge of her bed staring at it. I squeezed the envelope open where it had been slit across the top and saw the letter. I could tell there were several folded pages, all with the same neat handwriting as the address on the outside.

I sat and thought for a long time. It was Mama's letter, not mine. I thought about how I'd feel if Mama discovered the secret hiding place I had and read something private of mine. I'd be really mad. And what did it matter if I read it now, anyhow? I'd already written my letter, and Robert had mailed it. I stood up and slipped Mama's letter back under the telephone book.

Someday, I thought, *I'll meet him. Then we can talk in person, and that will be better.* I smiled as I stood there with my hand on the phone book. *And I bet he's got green eyes*, I said to myself.

Then I sighed, and dragged myself back to my chores.

Mama was bound and determined to make me think twice about ever fighting again. When she was home, we sat down and talked about things I could do to control my temper, like counting or trying to come up with something really helpful to say. I said I'd try, but finding something helpful to say to Dickie was going to be downright hard.

Every day Robert or Baby Blue stopped by to visit. We talked through the screen door. Robert told me about the new Head Start program Miss Woodruff had mentioned. It was starting up in lots of places around the country and was supposed to give kids an introduction to school. Beryl Ann was excited about it because Baby might qualify to attend.

I could tell Baby Blue was pretty excited, too. Every time he came by he took his thumb out of his mouth without being told to, long enough to tell me that he was going to go to school. Then his pale blue eyes would light up like Christmas lights.

Robert, too, was already looking forward to school starting, and it was just July!

The only thing I missed about school in the summer was not seeing Mr. Prichard, our favorite teacher, and not getting to go down to the little library in the school's old janitor's closet once a week to pick out a book to read.

I wasn't as much of a reader as Robert, but I'd read a whole bunch of books already. I'd read *Swiss Family Robinson* and all the Hardy Boys and Nancy Drew books the school had, and I was working my way through the books by Edgar Rice Burroughs and Jules Verne. Sometimes I thought about the future, like Jules Verne did. If I lived on another planet or in a big city under the sea, I could be a warrior princess and I wouldn't let bad guys like Dickie get away with anything—ever! And when I got mad, I wouldn't have to think about counting or about helpful things to say to mean people. I would just put them all in jail or exile all the bad people to their own undersea city, and that would be that.

On Monday, the day before the raffle drawing, Robert and Baby stopped by. Baby was wearing a pair of clean red jeans. "Where'd you get those?" I asked.

"Salvation Army," Baby said, smiling.

"We just got back from the Salvation Army store. Got some clothes," Robert said.

I noticed that he had on some white sneakers that looked pretty good. "New shoes," I said.

"Yup."

"So what else's new?" I asked.

"Miss Woodruff and a social worker are coming today to make arrangements for Baby to go to that Head Start school," Robert said.

"Great."

"He'll get a checkup, too, Mama said. They'll pay for him to get his teeth and eyes looked at."

For some reason, Robert didn't sound so happy about that. "That's good, isn't it?" I asked.

"Guess so," he said. "Only Daddy's not doing so good today, and they said they've got to come out and see the house and talk to him, too." Robert scratched at his bare shoulder, under the strap of his bib overalls, and pushed up on his glasses.

Uh-oh. When Robert said "not doing so good," it usually meant that Doyle was drunk. I could just picture Beryl Ann rushing round to get everything prettied up, and Doyle drunk on a bed in the front room. The Ketchums didn't have but two rooms and a toilet. There was a big old kitchen with a wood-burning stove, and a front room that had two beds, a couch, and a small coal-burning stove. They did have a nice big front porch, though.

"Maybe they'll sit out on the front porch with your mama, and they can talk to your daddy later," I said.

"Maybe." Robert didn't sound very confident. "We gotta go back and meet Miss Woodruff and the social worker in about an hour."

"I can't come out yet," I said. "And I'm not going to be able to go to the raffle drawing tomorrow. Do you think you could go to represent us in case we win?"

"Won't Adam tell us if they draw one of the slips he put in?"

"I suppose so." I hesitated. "But if you don't have to keep an eye on Baby, you could take my bike. Then you can get there and back really, really fast and let me know what happens. I'm just dying to know as soon as possible."

"I guess I could, if you got air in your tires," he said.

"I got air."

"You don't always. Half the time I have to keep them pumped up for you."

"Well, they've got air now."

"OK," he agreed, "if I don't have to take Baby." Then he pulled out a book from his back pocket and sat down on the back step to read.

That's Robert for you. Whenever he can, he opens up a book and loses himself in it. Most of the time I don't mind, because he likes to tell me the whole story later. And sometimes he even acts the stories out.

"That a good one?" I asked.

"Yup."

I watched him raise the book up high to his eyes and swing his head from left to right. Almost a whole week had passed and I hadn't yet come up with a plan to get money for Robert's glasses. This wasn't good. If I needed something really badly, I knew he would help me. And he had helped me by mailing out my secret letter to Dr. Harrison. So now I had to think of some way to help him.

While Robert read and Baby sat in Mama's freshly hoed garden and got his new pants dirty, I went back to my chores. But I was giving everything a hard think. I thought as I mopped the kitchen, and I thought as I scrubbed the bathroom walls for about the umpteenth time. Mama had sworn she could still see mold. I'd told her Mr. Prichard said that mold was a living thing, and maybe it had a right to live, too? But she wasn't buying that. So I scrubbed and I kept turning the problem over and over in my head.

After I finished scrubbing, I counted the change in my Smokey Bear bank: sixty-seven cents. I looked around my room. There wasn't anything I could part with, or that would bring more than a dollar even if I did sell it. And then I looked at the seashell bed lamp with twelve different kinds of shells, two flamingos, and one toucan that Grandma had brought back from a trip to Atlantic City. Grandma. *Hmm.* I wondered what my chances were of getting any money out of the Ol' Biddy.

ten

ON TUESDAY MORNING, after Mama had gone over to check on Lester, Robert stopped by. As soon as I came to the door, I knew something was up. I'd never seen him so twitchy in my life. He hopped from one foot to the other and kept hitching up on his pants and pushing up on his glasses.

"I got a new picture from Miss Woodruff," he announced. "Johnny Cash. I showed her the clubhouse and our collection when she was at the house yesterday. And she remembered she had a magazine in her car with Johnny Cash's picture in it. She's nice."

"That's great!" I said. "We don't have a Johnny Cash yet."

Robert and I had our own private clubhouse in the old tobacco-drying shed the Ketchums had out back. We'd furnished it with a couple of wooden chairs from my house and a red Coca-Cola cooler that we used as a table. It didn't work anymore, so Lester had given it to us. Inside the cooler we kept our library: our club logbook, an old dictionary we found by the school incinerator with no cover on it, and the books that Beryl Ann sometimes picked up from the county library for Robert.

Best of all, we had our collection. On every wall, as high up as we could reach, were pictures of movie stars and singers. So far we had seventy-eight. It was kind of hard to collect them, too, because Robert's family didn't get any magazines delivered, and the only one we subscribed to was *Reader's Digest*. But any time one of us went to the doctor's or someplace where there were magazines lying around, we always asked if we could tear out the pages with pictures of the stars. Most of the time they just let us have the old ones or tore out the pages for us. And every week Lester gave us his television guide from the Sunday *Bartlettsville Bugle* after he was done with it. On the very last page of each issue was a full-size picture of a movie star.

My job was to write down the name of each new star in the logbook, and Robert's job was to hang the picture. We'd pounded nails all over for the pictures. Doyle swore that place would never fall down because we had it so nailed up.

"Johnny Cash can go up by Elvis and the Beatles," I told Robert. "I'll come over and write it in the logbook as soon as I can." Then I waited, wondering what was upsetting him.

"I can't go into Hiram today," he said, "because Miss Woodruff and the social worker are coming back. I guess my daddy's got to sign some school papers for Baby, and he wasn't up to it yesterday."

"Oh, no!" I groaned. "That means I've got to wait until tomorrow to find out if we've won anything."

I wondered if I could sweet-talk Mama into letting me go to the drawing myself. After all, tomorrow was the last day of my official grounding and I'd done almost all the chores on her list. I'd even found a few things she hadn't listed and done them, too.

Thinking hard, I drummed my fingers on the door frame as I stared at the peeling paint. Then I heard Robert say something about "fit living conditions."

"What's that?" I asked him.

"This Mr. Ritchey, the social worker who was with Miss Woodruff yesterday, asked Mama if she thought she was providing 'fit living conditions' for us kids."

"What did your mama say?"

"She got really quiet and told him it was the fittin'est we had. I didn't like that Mr. Ritchey much. He tried to poke around the house. Then he kept asking if Daddy was *really* feeling poorly. He asked so many times that Daddy finally yelled out to the porch for him to shut his claptrap so's a body could get some rest. Now they're coming back today and I can't go to Hiram. But I like Miss Woodruff. She said she might have some more pictures for us now that she knows we collect them."

Well, I didn't like the sound of this Mr. Ritchey one bit. Who did he think he was, anyway? I was just getting worked up to tell Robert so when he leaned forward and whispered, "And Daddy—he took off this morning. I don't know if he'll be back in time to sign those papers. I've never seen my mama so mad!"

My mouth dropped open and I stared at Robert. I didn't think anyone had *ever* seen Beryl Ann mad. She wasn't born for it. My mama said Beryl Ann was born with a set of the sweetest bones God ever gave a body. She's big and as towheaded and blue-eyed as Baby. And when she hugs you, it's like being squeezed by the best-smelling pillows in the whole wide world.

It's kind of funny to see Beryl Ann and Doyle together, because Doyle's as thin as a rake and has to wear his pants belted on tight to keep them up. Maybe that's why he's so ornery to everybody except Baby. Maybe there just isn't room in him for any sweetness the way there is in Beryl Ann.

"What are you gonna do?" I asked, stepping out on the porch even though I wasn't supposed to. This was bad. Baby Blue would be crushed if he couldn't get into that special school. "Where'd your daddy go?"

"He waited till Mama went out to the vegetable garden, and told me he was just going up the road a piece. But that was more than two hours ago." Looking kind of shaky, Robert sat down on the top step.

I sat down next to him and put my hand on his shoulder. "If he's not there, can't they just come back again?" I asked, looking up into his face.

"Miss Woodruff said the deadline's real soon and we have to get all of Baby's paperwork into Bartlettsville as quick as possible."

Robert shook my hand off and stood back up. He straightened his shoulders and started down the steps. "Where are you going?" I asked him.

"Someone's gotta find Daddy." He looked up the road for a minute. "I'm going to the Howling Kitty."

"Robert! You *can't* go there. You know what kind of place that is! There's... there's... naked ladies and... and bad people. It's dangerous. You've heard Preacher Beaumont say so. Besides, kids aren't allowed in bars. It's against the law!"

"They'll be at the house soon, and Mama's cleaning Baby up now. I have to."

I watched as he stepped off into the grass, took the shortcut across our vacant field, and headed up the road. I couldn't believe it. Robert was going to the Howling Kitty!

Well, I couldn't wait for Mama to get home for lunch to talk to her. I zipped through the last chore she had listed. Then I grabbed the list, ran out, jumped on my bike, and rode over to the Gas & Go.

Mama looked up, surprised to see me. I shoved the list at her. At the bottom I'd written all the extra chores I'd done during the week. I said, "Tomorrow's my last day of being grounded. And since I've done everything on your list, and even some extra chores, I was wondering if I could get off a little early. There's something important going on in Hiram this afternoon and—"

"Honey"—she stopped me—"there's *never* anything important going on in Hiram."

"The Rotary is drawing for its raffle, and I want to go see who wins."

"Is that all?"

I hemmed and hawed, not really wanting to answer that last question, as she picked up the list and looked it over. "Well," Mama said, studying it, "I'm not sure we can really count exercising Mr. Perkins as an extra chore."

"You're always saying how he's getting fat, so I made him jump ten times this morning. And—"

"OK, OK," she said, laughing and holding up one hand. "This is great, sweetie. I guess you *have* made a special effort. But no more fighting. We're agreed, yes?"

"Yes. I...I promise to count to ten before I get angry with anything someone says, even if it's mean or stupid. And I'll...I'll ignore them and I won't let it get to me. And I'll try to use words instead of my fists if I absolutely *must* do something. And . . . and, I'll try to say something helpful, if I can think of anything." I put my hand over my heart and started to push open the Gas & Go's screen door with my rear end.

"If you're riding your bike to Hiram, you be careful."

"Yes, ma'am!" I shouted, and raced over to my bike as I heard the screen door slam shut behind me.

I truly *was* going into Hiram. I just had to go to the Howling Kitty first.

eleven

I WAS PEDALING SO FAST that the rear wheel of my bike slid over some loose gravel when I turned out of our driveway. At the same time, I looked over my shoulder to make sure no cars were coming and saw Lester waving from his front porch. I figured I'd go see him soon as I got things sorted out.

I leaned low over the handlebars, my face slicing into the wind. At the fork in the road past the Ketchum place, instead of going straight on to Hiram I made a hard left turn and headed out along the river bottom toward Bartlettsville and the Howling Kitty bar. The Howling Kitty is at least three miles up the road, and I thought I had a good chance of catching up with Robert, since he was walking.

The road along the Little Red River is about the flattest place in Beulah County, so it wasn't hard pedaling. As I rode, I breathed in the sweet, heavy smell of growing things that always lingered there by the river.

What if they wouldn't let Robert in to talk to Doyle? What if he did talk to Doyle, but Doyle wouldn't leave and go home? What if they called the police? That wouldn't look good to Mr. Ritchey, the social worker.

Finally, I came around a curve and there it was, an old cement-block building painted bright pink, with a few scraggly bushes growing up along its sides. The sign reading HOWLING KITTY hung crookedly from a pole in a cement base out front, so that the woman on the sign with a tiger mask on seemed to be howling at the ground. There was a tipped-over garbage can just below. Doyle's beat-up blue pickup truck with a missing front fender was parked by the garbage can. Around the back, a couple of old cars sat up on blocks, patiently waiting for some part that was never going to arrive.

I lowered my bike onto the gravel and stepped around it. I hadn't passed Robert on the road, and I didn't see him now. So that meant he was inside, if he hadn't changed his mind about coming here.

I'd never been to a bar before. Was I supposed to knock? Would someone come to the door and peek out at me through a tiny window at the top of the door, like they do in gangster movies? I ran up to the door and stopped. I didn't see a tiny window.

I decided to open the door and look in. That way, even if they did kick me out, I could see if Robert was there. I took a deep breath and slowly pulled the door open.

It was dark inside, like going into a picture show. For a few moments I couldn't see a thing. Then I heard a deep voice. "Not another one! You stay out of here. You can't come in here."

I stepped in, squinting in the darkness. "Is Robert here?"

"Here I am," said Robert's voice. When I could finally see well enough to make out something, I saw him standing up front. And hunched over a table, about a foot away, sat Doyle.

Well, there weren't any naked ladies, and I didn't see the devil "in-carnated," as Preacher Beaumont says, but I sure was shaking all over.

"If you're looking for the other kid, you've found him. Now get the hell out of here, the both of you."

The gruff voice came from a man in a green striped shirt pulled tight over his big arms and bulging belly. He was standing behind a long shiny counter near Doyle's table.

"OK," I managed to croak, "just let me get my friend." Then I stumbled my way past empty chairs to Robert. "C'mon." I grabbed his arm. "We gotta get out of here."

"I can't unless he comes, too." Robert nodded toward Doyle.

"I'm busy!" yelled Doyle, lifting his head unsteadily from the table. "Ain't I done told you already? I'll be home later. Now git."

"You've got to come with me *now*," said Robert. "Mama needs you at home."

"I'm your father, dammit! You're supposed to do what I say. And I said to get your sorry butt home. You hear me, boy? Go!" Doyle turned round in his chair and reached out toward Robert.

Robert scooted a little beyond arm's length from his father and stood looking down at the floor with his hands in his pockets. I watched as he slowly and steadily breathed in and out. I held my breath. "No," he answered.

Oh, no. I thought for sure Doyle was going to jump up and take off after him with his belt. But he just groaned and put his head back down on his arms. Robert didn't move a lick.

"OK, that's it," shouted the bartender, slapping both his hands down on the countertop. "I'm calling the sheriff. They'll haul *all* your sorry butts home. You'll not get me in trouble for letting you in here."

The last thing I wanted, after just finishing a week of being grounded, was to go and get myself hauled home by the police. "C'mon, Robert," I hissed. "He's calling the police."

"That's OK. You go," he said. "I can't."

"Kids," I heard Doyle mutter to himself. "You try your dam'dest, and they still grow up without a bit of respect these days. Where's my little Baby, huh? You watching out for him? He's the only one...listens to me."

I backed up to the door. "You sure?" I asked.

Robert nodded.

So I turned and ran back out and jumped on my bike. I rode down the road a ways and into the cornfield across on the other side to wait. It wasn't too long before the county sheriff's car pulled in. A few minutes later Doyle came staggering out, held up by an officer and followed by Robert. I guess Doyle was too drunk to drive, because they all got in the police car and headed back toward Baylor. Robert looked out the window at me as they drove by.

twelve

I TURNED MY BIKE around and took off for Hiram, amazed at how calm Robert had seemed. I don't know how he did it. If I had a father like Doyle and had to go to a bar to get him, I'd be spitting mad.

Sometimes I wondered why Robert bothered with Doyle at all. I mean, even though I was hoping to meet Dr. Harrison soon, I had been doing just fine, so far, without a father. The only thing I knew that Doyle ever did for Robert was to let him use the old tobacco shed for our clubhouse. Also he gave us the nails to hang up our pictures. The way I looked at it, that just wasn't enough.

Doyle hadn't even signed those papers to get Baby into Head Start. But the most amazing thing was that Beryl Ann had gotten mad. I just couldn't picture *that* at all, not at all!

By the time I got to Hiram it was already 2:30. I went straight to the hardware store. Adam was working on a display of hand tools. "Well?" I asked.

"Well?"

"*You* know. The drawing's at three o'clock. Are you gonna go and watch?"

"Hmm." He smiled and shook his head. "We're pretty busy right now. I'm not sure I can make it."

I looked around the store. There wasn't a soul in sight. "C'mon, Adam, quit teasing! We've got at least two chances to win. I'm going over to watch even if you aren't."

"Hold your horses. Let me finish this and tell my uncle where I'm going." He stacked one last pair of pliers on the shelf and came out from behind the counter. "The drawing's not until three, and it must be—oh, let me see—at least a two-minute walk across the street to the bank. Can't start out too early, I guess."

I rolled my eyes. "I just want to get a good seat, that's all. But take your time." I pretended to yawn, and poked around in a box full of red hose spigots.

Adam finally headed for the door. "You never know when you might need a good spigot," he said with a laugh.

He took such long steps that I had to run to catch up to him as he crossed the street. He was whistling while we walked down two doors to the First Farmers and Tenants Bank.

"Adam, if you had a choice, would you rather have no father at all or one that wasn't any good?" I asked him.

Adam stopped by the door of the bank. "That's a hard question, Jessie." He looked away a minute, thinking.

"Let's see. . . . I guess it would depend on a lot of things," he said. "For instance, what's the rest of the family like? I mean, if the rest of a family—the mother, brothers, sisters, aunts and uncles, and others—are really loving, they can help fill up an empty place in someone's heart or heal a hurt caused by a no-account parent. But it also depends upon how bad this parent is. If they're just lazy or shiftless, that's one thing. But if they're mean or *really* bad, that's a whole other can of worms, so to speak."

I could tell Adam was watching someone behind me as he talked, so I turned and looked around. Dickie's daddy was up by the Hiram Feed & Seed. "Take him, for instance," said Adam, nodding in Mr. Whitten's direction. "Now, Curtis Whitten is one man I wouldn't wish on any poor child as a father."

I watched Mr. Whitten rear back and spit a spray of brown tobacco juice out of the side of his mouth and onto the granite stone below the Feed & Seed window as he pushed open the door. He hadn't even tried to aim for the dented spittoon that sat there.

Mr. Whitten was known to have a really mean streak in him. He had even lit into Preacher Beaumont one day outside the church. Everyone thought it was going to come to a fistfight, but they'd dragged Mr. Whitten away.

The talk around town was that Dickie's daddy was a snake handler and attended a Church with Signs, a "handler's church," up on the mountainside, talking and dancing with poisonous snakes. Snake handling wasn't exactly legal, but some folks did it anyway, even some otherwise pretty nice and ordinary folks. But others here in town said it was dangerous and stupid. It was kind of like making 'shine. Some people did that, too. In fact, there was a rumor that Mr. Whitten ran a moonshine still up behind his place.

So folks weren't supposed to know about the snake

handlers. But almost everyone knew that Mr. Whitten, and others from over by Bartlettsville, worshiped by the taking up of serpents. Dickie had even bragged at school as how his daddy kept a pet diamondback named Ol' One Eye, and how he was going to let Dickie handle him soon. But none of us believed him. Dickie was always full of big talk.

Every so often we would hear that the sheriff had made a run up the back of Martin's Mountain in the middle of the night to break up a handler gathering. But it never stopped for long. Pretty soon there'd be talk of the handlers getting together again.

It had never occurred to me to think about what kind of father Dickie had, or to wonder whether Mr. Whitten was crazy or just plain mean, like Dickie.

Adam was already stepping through the First Farmers door. Inside, the bank looked about the same as it always does, one or two people in line. A couple of the women who worked there started talking to Adam. He always seemed to gather a group of women wherever he went. I think most of the single women around here were glad when he came back from Michigan to help his uncle with the hardware store. I sat down on one of the wooden benches by the door to wait.

By the time of the drawing, a crowd of almost twenty was milling about, including DeeDee Byrum, her mama, and her daddy, the banker. Mr. Salyer, Missy's daddy, was the president of the Rotary, so he was going to be the one to pull the slips from the box. But first he gave a little speech about supporting local business and how this was the tenth year for the Hiram raffle and how it raised money for the community.

Adam and I stood together watching as he reached in for the name of the third-prize winner. Third prize was a free permanent wave at Debbie's Dos, a new beauty parlor in town. That went to Mrs. Daniels, who giggled as she stepped forward.

Then Mr. Salyer reached in to get the name for the second prize, the one I wanted: a gift certificate to the Roadside Grill. I crossed my fingers. I closed my eyes. I repeated over and over to myself, "*Please* let it be Adam's slip. Please let it be..."

No such luck. Second prize went to DeeDee's mother, Mrs. Byrum. She laughed and shook everybody's hand as she went up for her gift certificate. I glowered at DeeDee. What the heck did they need that for? Mr. and Mrs. Byrum were rich and could go to the Roadside Grill whenever they felt like it.

I wanted to leave right then. I tugged at Adam's shirt and nodded toward the door. He reached out, took my hand, squeezed it, and shook his head. So we stayed for the whole thing.

First prize was a choice of $20 worth of auto parts from one of Mr. Salyer's auto dealerships. Mr. Salyer drew the slip and announced that first prize went to Mr. Buggs, the church organist in Baylor, which wasn't going to do him any good because he didn't own a car. But judging by the number of chins his face creased into, he seemed pleased.

"Let's go," I whispered to Adam. This whole thing was pitiful. I wished I hadn't wasted fifty cents by entering.

But then Mr. Salyer held up his hands to quiet the crowd

and announced that they were going to draw for a consolation prize. I wondered what that was going to be when suddenly Adam let go of my hand and stepped forward. Mr. Salyer must have called his name, though I didn't hear him do it. I held my breath while Adam thanked everybody and came back to stand beside me. Then Mr. Salyer made a short thank-you speech and folks began to leave.

"What'd we win?" I asked.

"Let's see," said Adam, reading the fancy certificate. "It says, 'Redeemable for five dollars' worth of supplies at the Hiram Feed and Seed Store.'"

"Feed and Seed! What good is that? I'm not a farmer, and neither are you. Some consolation." I turned and stomped out the door, not waiting for Adam.

thirteen

I RODE MY BIKE to the Ketchums'. I had to find out if Robert had gotten into trouble for going to the Howling Kitty. And I had to give him the bad news about the raffle. It just seemed like nothing was going right lately. Certainly, neither of our mamas was going to get a night out.

At the Ketchums' I got off my bike and wound my way past the hubcaps to the porch steps. Nobody was out in the yard, and I didn't see Doyle's truck. It was probably still at the Howling Kitty. I leaned my bike against the house and started up the steps.

I could see through the wood-framed screen door to the front room, where Robert was sitting in a chair.

I was going to call out, but something held me back. Maybe it was the way he sat in the chair. Maybe it was the stillness of the place.... Maybe it was the hand I saw reaching out to clasp Robert's like it was hanging on for dear life.

I couldn't move. I stood there watching Robert sit with his head down, holding his father's hand. How could he? Then I turned and slipped quietly back down the steps.

I'd rarely seen Doyle do anything but sleep, curse, and occasionally play with Baby. It seemed like Doyle hardly even knew he had an older son. Robert and I, we were...well, it had always been kind of like we were the same—that neither one of us had a father.

Now Doyle had gone and messed things up good.

I grabbed my bike and rode down the road to Lester's house. A funny tight feeling was growing in my chest. It had been a long, long day.

"Lester!" I yelled. I pushed open the back door and walked in without waiting to be invited.

Lester was sitting in his favorite reclining chair by the big front window where he could see his bird feeders. He smiled when he saw me and said, "Little one!" And then he took a good look up and down at me, and opened up his arms.

I climbed up onto the arm of his chair and sat with my cheek against the top of his head. We watched the few birds that stopped by and didn't talk for a long time. It felt good.

Finally, I leaned back and looked at his wrinkled cheeks and his white hair, which still curled over his ears. "So, how're you feeling?" I asked. "Mama says I'm not to pester you. She said that more than once."

He shook his head and laughed. "You never pester me, little one."

Lester's called me "little one" for as far back as I can remember. And even though I'm hardly little anymore and can barely fit in his chair with him now, that's still OK by me.

"I'm doing a mite better today," he said. "Just a bad bout

with the ol' rheumatiz. Doc says to sit in the sunshine and pray that it stays dry for a spell. Anyhow, I'm much better now that you're here." He looked at me all serious-like. "While I seem to be getting handsomer every day, you look like something the cat drug in."

"Yeah. I know. It's been a bad day; a whole bad week, Lester."

I gulped down that tight feeling in my throat and chest and told him all about it. He listened, nodding every so often and exclaiming, "My, my!" when I got to the part about the Howling Kitty bar. I told him about Doyle drinking a lot lately and not helping Baby get into the Head Start school, about Robert not getting new glasses, about Grandma getting divorced again, and even about fighting with Dickie. I told him about everything except the letter to Dr. Harrison. For some reason, I didn't want to talk about that. That was my personal secret. And I didn't say anything about what I'd just seen at Robert's.

"Hmm, hmm, hmm," Lester sighed. "That Doyle, if he keeps up his drinking, he's either going to kill himself or someone else one of these days. I remember when he was just a dirt-streaked kid and he played with my grandson, Jack. They were about the same age. Lord, how his daddy used to beat him. Sometimes we'd see Old Man Ketchum going up the road with a switch, taking off through the woods after young Doyle." Lester shook his head. "The funny thing is, his old man was a temperance man. Didn't have no truck with the bottle at all. And now his son's living in one. Old Man Ketchum wasn't worth two cents in my opinion—no kind of father. Well, the Good Book says, 'Ye reap what ye sow.' And to my way of thinking, just because a man plants a seed in the ground, it doesn't make him a farmer. He's got to tend the crop, too. That's the most important part."

We watched the birds for a few minutes, and then Lester continued, "The thing is, I think down deep Doyle's not so bad if he could stay off the bottle. The best thing Doyle ever did with his life was to marry Beryl Ann."

I got twitchy listening to Lester talk about Doyle, and I didn't want to think about the way Doyle had been holding onto Robert so tight. I climbed down from Lester's chair and made my usual rounds of his living room. I liked touching his things, his pictures in their old frames, and his pipes that he doesn't smoke anymore. I've always touched them lightly, with just the tip of my finger. There was something about how old everything was, how it had all been there forever. Each and every thing seemed to have its own special spot in the world, even all the old books and magazines he kept stacked up around the place. Lester reads a whole lot, maybe even more than Robert.

I liked the photographs best, at least most of them. It was nice just to have some photographs around; we didn't have *any* from before our house burned down. Lester looked happy in the ones with his daughter, Darlene, and his wife, Alantha. The only one I didn't like was the one of his grandson, Jack. He didn't look nice, not like Lester at all.

Lester said, "I wouldn't worry about Baby Blue and that special school. Miss Woodruff's a go-getter. She'll be sure to get him in and get all the papers done up right, even if Doyle does give her a hard time. Nice woman; she's got her head and her heart in the right places."

"How'd she know we needed help?" I asked. "I know she's a VISTA volunteer and working for the government and all that. But how'd she know to come *here* in the first place?"

Lester slowly got up from his chair. I handed him his cane. "Darn leg," he whispered. And then louder, "I need me a deep-thinking drink. How about you?"

He went out the back door and pushed off the lid to the well at the edge of the back porch. Then he dropped in his old wooden bucket and hauled it back up. Oh, Lester has running water like we do, and an inside toilet. But he likes well water best and keeps the old well in good repair. He claims water from the tap is hardly fit for humans to drink, and that a swig of good well water—or even better, cold mountain spring water—clears the head and lets a body think.

After we both had a long cool drink from the metal ladle, Lester said, as he always did, "Ahh, the best water in the world."

"Yup." I nodded, smiling, and answered as I always did, "The best water in the world."

"Actually," Lester continued as he turned to go back in, "I'd already read about the president's War on Poverty and those VISTA volunteers before Miss Woodruff got here. It's a good thing overall, I think. Come here, let me show you something."

We walked back into the house. In several corners of the

kitchen were piles of magazines and newspapers. "Scrounge around through there. About a week or two ago I brought home a *New York Times* somebody gave me. Should be there somewhere."

After a few minutes of digging through the pile, I found the newspaper. We opened it on the kitchen table. In the second section was an article about "the rural poor" and VISTA volunteers. Also there was a big picture right in the middle of the page. It was of a coal miner coming home, just the pale rings of his eyes and his white teeth shining out of his blackened face. In one hand he toted his lunch pail. The other hand was clasped onto a young one about Baby's age, barefoot and dressed only in a ripped pair of underwear. A whole passel of young ones waited on the porch.

"It's articles like this that gets folks like Miss Woodruff wanting to come and help," Lester said.

"Old Joe at the hardware store called Miss Woodruff 'an up-North do-gooder.'"

"You know, VISTA stands for Volunteers in Service to America," he said. "Well, Miss Woodruff told me they volunteer to help people right here in America with things like schooling and getting folks their medical checkups and shots."

"I know that part already," I said. "What I want to know is, why'd she pick *Baylor* to come to?"

"She told me she'd seen some news recently on the TV and in the Cincinnati papers about the mines closing around here. So after she retired from working as a school administrator up North and there was an opportunity for her to come here, she said she didn't have to think twice about it," Lester said. "And I heard she's getting some things done already. She's getting kids registered for school early with this special Head Start program, like she's trying to do for Baby Blue. Also, she's taking the miners' kids from Greasy Ridge into Hiram in her own car so they can get their shots free and be ready for school, come fall. It's good that folks get riled up and want to help."

"Doyle seems to be riled up something awful lately, and that isn't helping anybody, especially Baby," I pointed out.

Lester sighed. "Well, that's a different kind of riled up. He's out of work, too, and probably feeling pretty touchy about out-of-town folks poking around."

He paused and rubbed his stubbly jaw. "You see, it's hard on a man when he can't support his family in the way that he thinks he ought to. A man can get mighty ashamed of that. So Doyle, and others, get mad at do-gooders who come nosing around what they think of as their personal business. They end up losing their tempers and not taking advantage of things that're to their own benefit. But if something good can come out of it, like Baby going to Head Start, where he can learn all kinds of things and get to the doctor's, isn't it worth it? And," he added, pointing to the picture, "the other good thing is that some of these people, maybe they'll get five or ten dollars from photographers for letting their pictures get taken. Five dollars would go a long way toward feeding some families for a week, and ten dollars would help pay the rent for a month for some folks."

"Why would anybody pay so much just for a picture?" I

asked. "Shoot! They could take *my* picture for less than that, if I was cleaned up first."

"These writers, reporters, and photographers, they have reputations to keep up by showing what's happening around the world, like it really is. They don't want pretty snapshots with folks in their Sunday hats. They're all trying to make us sadder, or madder than a hornet, so we'll get up off our backsides and do something brave to make things change for the good, like Miss Woodruff."

"Brave?" I asked. I'd thought that Miss Woodruff was just nice and all.

"Sure," said Lester. "She came down here all by herself. Some folks welcomed her, and some folks, like Doyle, are downright mean and ornery to her. It takes a lot of gumption to do that. Miss Woodruff isn't a spring chicken, either." Lester shook his head. "But when something's really important to a person, you'd be surprised how brave that person can be—like Robert today. It sounds like he was pretty brave, too."

Robert, brave? I'd never thought about him that way before. I'd always liked how Robert didn't let things get him all twisted up inside. But I hadn't thought about that as Robert's way of being brave. Maybe Lester was right.

I hugged him and left for home, pushing my bike across the road.

fourteen

THE NEXT MORNING I GOT up early, before Mama, grabbed a cold biscuit from yesterday's dinner, and headed out. I walked over to Robert and Baby's, jumping over the bright blue chicory flowers along the side of the road. Over my shoulder I could see some fog lying sleepily above the river. I might have been the only one up in all of Baylor.

I'd had a hard time falling to sleep the night before. I kept waking up with a tightness in my throat. But I did decide something; sometimes you *do* have to grab onto a problem and wrestle it to the ground. Sometimes there just isn't any escaping it. Lester had convinced me. If Robert and Miss Woodruff could be brave and try to change things, so could I.

First, I had to find out what happened when Robert got home yesterday. Then I had to knuckle down and figure out how to get the money for his glasses.

I crept up onto the Ketchums' front porch and over to the window above Robert and Baby's bed. I crouched down and raised myself just enough to peek over the windowsill. It looked like everybody was still abed. "Robert," I whispered.

Nothing happened. *"Rob-bert,"* I said a little louder and lightly tapped my fingers on the windowpane.

Suddenly, a pale face popped up. It was Baby Blue, with his thumb in his mouth. I pressed my face to the window and pointed over to Robert. The next thing I knew, Baby Blue was pushing open the front door. He was dressed only in his underpants.

"Baby," I whispered, "did Robert get into trouble yesterday?"

Baby shook his head. Then he took his thumb out of his mouth and with a big smile said, "Police car came to our house yesterday!"

I knelt down and hugged him. "I know. But you're sure? Robert didn't get into trouble?"

Again Baby shook his head.

"Good!"

Then Baby said, "I'm going to school, too, Jessie."

"You are?"

"Yup. Mama and the nice lady said so."

"They did? Was this just yesterday, Baby? *After* the police car?"

"Yup," Baby said again, nodding his head up and down.

"That's great!" I jumped off the porch and did a cartwheel on the dirt.

Baby followed me as I headed to the clubhouse, which was back behind the Ketchums' coal pile. Once inside, I sat down and put my feet up on the cooler. Baby put his feet up, too. It was cool and quiet there in the early morning.

I looked at all the bright smiling faces around me:

Elizabeth Taylor, Danny Kaye, Elvis, Lucille Ball, Debbie Reynolds, the Beatles, Bob Hope, and now Johnny Cash. I couldn't keep from smiling myself. This was great. Baby was getting into Head Start, after all.

I got out the logbook and put Johnny Cash's name in it and the date. I flipped through the book. "See, Baby. Our collection is really growing. Someday, when we hit one hundred, we'll celebrate!"

"I can count to one hundred," Baby said.

"You can?"

"Yup," he said. And then he did.

So we played school for a while. We went through all the ABCs, and even got out one of Robert's library books and read a little. I'd never heard Baby Blue talk so much at one time.

After a while he slid off his chair. "I'm hungry," he said, and slipped out the door. I figured it was about breakfast time and was thinking about heading home myself when Robert showed up.

"Hey," he said, stepping through the door. "Baby said you were out here."

"Yeah. I wanted to put Johnny Cash in the logbook." I picked the logbook up to show him the new entry.

Robert took the logbook, held it up close, and smiled as he studied it. Then he closed it and said, "So...thanks for...well, for coming to the Howling Kitty yesterday."

"What happened after you got home? All Baby said was that he was going to go to school."

"Well," said Robert, "Officer Boyd drove me and Daddy home. Miss Woodruff was on the porch with Mama and Mr.

Ritchey, the social worker. When we got out of the police car, Mr. Ritchey turned all red, like he was gonna explode. But Miss Woodruff, she just stepped right up to Daddy and slapped those school papers into his hands and handed him a pen. Officer Boyd stayed while Mama and Daddy went inside and talked. After a good while Mama came back out with everything signed, I guess, and handed it all back to Miss Woodruff."

"You never got a whipping for going into the Howling Kitty?" I asked.

"Nope. Officer Boyd took Daddy around to the back of the house where I think he did a lot of talking and Daddy did a lot of listening. I did hear him say Daddy wasn't to go back for the truck until he was . . . better. After that"—Robert shrugged—"Daddy went into the house and fell asleep. He slept for the rest of the day and he's still in bed."

"That's good," I said.

Robert pulled an envelope out of his back pocket. "Here. I got something for you. Adam came around later looking for you when he couldn't find you at your house or the Gas and Go."

"I was at Lester's yesterday after the raffle." I didn't say anything about stopping by Robert's house first. "But if it's about the raffle, forget it. We won a consolation prize— five dollars' worth of feed and seed. Fat lot of good that'll do either of us, unless your mama wants to use it for her garden."

He handed me the envelope. "Here. Open it."

I opened it, and inside was five dollars. "What!"

"Adam said his Uncle Joe wanted the feed and seed, so he swapped him five dollars for the gift certificate. So now his uncle can get his seed, and we've got five dollars!" Robert was smiling.

I couldn't help jumping and shouting, "Whoopee! Yes, sir! Yes, sir! *Yes, sir!*" I danced around the clubhouse, then went over and kissed Elvis, making Robert laugh. "This is great. It may still be enough for a date for my mama, what do you think?"

And then, while I stood there with that money in my hand, it hit me. "How do we know whose it is?" I asked. "Adam put in for both our mamas. Who should get the prize?"

Robert scratched the top of one bare foot with the bottom of the other one and said, "It doesn't matter. You paid for the raffle tickets, your mama should be the winner."

"No," I said firmly. "We should share it, or"—I caught the early morning sun glinting off Robert's old glasses—"we'll save it and put it toward something important we both want." I knew exactly what that was going to be.

Robert was going to argue with me. But then a shadow blocked the sunlight from the clubhouse door, and Doyle stumbled in.

Uh-oh! Why was he up so early? Was he just hung over or had he been drinking already? I slid the envelope with the money in it into my back pocket.

"Where's that five dollars?" he demanded, without a "Howdy" or a "Good morning."

"It's . . . it's . . ." Robert seemed surprised. He backed up by one of the clubhouse walls. "It's . . ."

"It's *my* money!" I shouted, wondering how Doyle knew about it. "It's mine and I'm keeping it."

"Shut your mouth, girl," Doyle said. "I know what's what. I heard Adam out on the porch yesterday. He said he didn't rightly know which one of you had won it. So I figured it was just as likely my boy's, and I'd get it bright and early this morning and put it to good use."

"It's mine. I asked Adam to enter for us, and I paid for the raffle tickets all by myself," I said. "You aren't getting it."

Doyle looked at me like thunder was writ clear across his face. Suddenly, he turned, took two steps across the clubhouse, and struck out with his open hand, slapping Robert up alongside his head so hard his glasses went flying. It would have knocked him right over, but he fell against the wall.

"Haven't I warned you about playing with girls all the time!" Doyle shouted and started to raise his hand again. "Here's another one for yesterday, too. It's time you learnt some respect."

"Stop that!" I screamed. "Stop it! I'm gonna go tell Beryl Ann!"

"You," Doyle growled, lowering his hand and turning back to me. "This ain't your business. This ain't your property. You get out of here before I throw you out myself. Then we'll see how many tales you'll be carrying."

I ran to the door and spun around. "You lay a hand on me and I'll scratch your eyes out," I spat back at him. Then I leaped out the door and ran and never stopped until I got home.

fifteen

I PUSHED THE KITCHEN DOOR open hard with both hands, feeling sure that my heart was going to bust wide open before I got inside. I went sliding across the slippery linoleum floor and landed—*thump!*—right on my fanny by the kitchen table. I looked up, and who was sitting there but Mama and Grandma. Grandma held a nail-polish brush, poised dead in midair. They were both looking bug-eyed around the end of the table and down at me. Somehow I hadn't even noticed Grandma's Thunderbird in the driveway.

"You OK, sweetie?" Mama asked.

I was shaking so much I couldn't talk at first. And it took me an awfully long time to get up off the floor. When I finally got on my feet, I put my hands down on the table and leaned over to catch my breath. "Doyle...Doyle just knocked Robert clear across the clubhouse. And he tried to take our money."

Mama pushed back her chair—hard. "Did he touch you? Did he hurt you?" she demanded.

"No, no." I shook my head. "Robert's glasses came flying off. And he wanted our money."

"What money?" Grandma asked.

I slipped my hand into my back pocket, pulled out the envelope with the five dollars in it, and slapped it down on the tabletop. Grandma put the nailbrush back in the red polish and opened the envelope.

"Robert and I won the consolation prize in the Rotary raffle," I said. "Adam brought it over yesterday. We're gonna save it for something special."

"You won this fair and square?" Grandma asked.

"Of course," I said. What'd she think, I'd stolen it?

Mama pushed her chair all the way out, went to the door, and slipped on her flip-flops. "I'm going over to see Beryl Ann," she said.

"Doyle's there," I warned her. "I don't know if he's drunk or not."

"I'm not afraid of Doyle," Mama said. "You stay here with your grandmother. I don't want you following me."

I glanced at Grandma. I wasn't sure I wouldn't rather be tagging along with Mama, even if Doyle was there, than staying here by myself with Grandma. She had returned to touching up her bright red fingernail polish. On the table in front of her was a cup of coffee and a brown paper shopping bag. I also noticed that she'd dyed her hair again, this time really dark, almost black. It made the white puffiness of her face stand out even more. And except for the sunglasses perched up on top of her head, she reminded me a bit of one of those half-dead zombies in the movies. It suddenly came to me that Grandma must work at looking so strange. She wasn't even that old for a grandma, considering Mama had only just turned twenty when she had me.

"OK," I whispered, and slipped into Mama's chair across the kitchen table from Grandma. I heard the door slam as Mama left.

Grandma kept her head bent, polishing her nails for a long time. I put my two hands palms down on the table and kind of drummed the tabletop a little with my thumbs, waiting. I knew Grandma would say something to me sooner or later. She was humming to herself as she fussed with her nails.

"Your hands could use some sprucing up, too," she finally said.

I looked at my hands. They were pretty grimy, and the nails were caked with dirt. "I was in a hurry this morning," I said.

"That so?" she answered, and cocked one eyebrow at me. "A girl should be more careful with her *toilette*. You never know who you might run into during the day."

"My what?" I asked.

"*Twa-let*," she pronounced slowly. "It's French. It means everything you do to get yourself cleaned up of a morning: washing, getting dressed, brushing your teeth."

"We don't speak French around here," I answered her. "Besides, who am I gonna run into except Robert or Baby Blue anyhow?"

"You never know," Grandma said. "Life is full of surprises.

See, I've even got a surprise for you, here in this bag." She pushed the paper sack across the table toward me and started blowing on her nails. Then she stopped and studied me. "Maybe you'd better wash your hands before you open it," she said.

Grandma had won that round. Though it really wasn't fair because she knew I'd want to see what was in the bag. I dragged myself over to the kitchen sink, washed my hands, and quickly dried them off on a towel. "Better?" I asked, flipping them over to show her both sides.

Grandma just snorted out her nose and watched me while I pulled the sack closer and opened it.

sixteen

I LOOKED AT THE white cotton contraption with elastic criss-crossing every which way through metal hooks and pulleys and a little pink bow dead center and could hardly believe it. I was not, absolutely not, *positively not,* going to get trussed up in a girl harness.

I don't remember everything I said to Grandma, but finally I yelled, "It isn't any of your business. So there!" And then I glared at her and crossed my arms. I'd had just about all of this pushy old woman I could take.

She yelled right back, "It *is* my business, and you'd better get used to it! So there!" She folded her arms, too.

Suddenly, I noticed Mama standing in the doorway. And she did the strangest thing. She looked from me to Grandma and started laughing. I'd never seen my mama laugh so hard. In fact, she started to slide down toward the floor.

I glared at her. "Mother!" What was wrong with her?

"Mirabelle!" demanded Grandma indignantly.

"I'm ... sorry," she gasped. "It's just that ..." and then she broke off into more peals of laughter. I could tell she was trying to get control. She said, "It's just that ... I'm sorry." And then she started up all over again. She held her side and, finally, bent over with tears in her eyes from laughing so hard, she said, "I think I might pee my pants. Oh!" She struggled to get into a chair. Then she put her head down and laughed so hard she shook the table.

I stamped my foot. "Mama!"

"Well, I don't see what's so funny," Grandma snapped. "Please enlighten us."

"I'm sorry. I'm sorry," Mama said, hiccupping and wiping at her tear-stained cheeks. "It's just that . . . you two just . . . two peas in a pod. Just alike, you two . . . two peas . . ."

I couldn't believe what Mama was saying. Us? Just alike? *Grandma* and me? Grandma and I were . . . well, we were as different as cats and dogs. Anybody could see that.

"Ridiculous!" Grandma said as she crossed her legs and turned her back to us. For once, I completely agreed with her. I stomped off down the hall. When I got to my bedroom, I slammed my door—extra hard.

After a while I stopped pacing back and forth across my room and quietly opened the door a crack. I could hear Mama and Grandma in the kitchen, their voices low. What were they talking about? And what had happened with Mama at the Ketchums'?

I hadn't had anything to eat except the cold biscuit, and I was starving. So I took a deep breath, left my bedroom, and walked calmly into the kitchen. I went over to the cupboard to get out the cereal without giving Mama or Grandma a direct look. In the middle of the table lay that *thing* Grandma had brought me. I didn't look at it, either.

I could tell they were watching me. I opened the fridge and poured some milk over my Puffed Wheat. I put a piece of bread in the toaster and sat down at the end of the table, between them, to eat my breakfast. No one said a word.

When I looked up from my cereal, I could see a smile twitching at the corners of Mama's mouth.

I cleared my throat and asked her, "So what happened when you went to see Beryl Ann?"

"Well," Mama began, "I was just going up their drive when I met Doyle heading out. He wasn't too happy to see me. He told me I wasn't welcome, and you weren't welcome at his house anymore."

"Oh, no!" I dropped my spoon. "What about Robert and Baby Blue? They're my best friends! I just—"

"Hush," Mama interrupted me, raising her palm up like she was directing traffic. "It'll be all right; that's just Doyle talking. I've got a feeling he isn't going to be around for a while—he was taking his things with him. He had his shotgun and a paper sack full of clothes under his arm. So I waited a bit and then went on up to the house to see Beryl Ann. It seems she told him to get out and not to come back until he'd done something about his drinking."

"You mean they're gonna get a divorce?" I gasped. I was amazed. Folks around here didn't get divorced, except Grandma, of course.

"I didn't say that," Mama said sharply. "And don't go talking about this to anyone else. Beryl Ann just said that she told Doyle she didn't want to set eyes on him again unless he was sober and getting help to stay that way. And he isn't to raise a hand to Robert or Baby either, or go near them, or she'll call the police."

"About time," Grandma chimed in. "Good riddance to bad rubbish, I say."

"Mama!" objected my mother.

And what about Baby, I wondered. For some reason, he loved his daddy. It used to be that if Doyle was sober and up and around, Baby followed him everywhere. Unfortunately, that wasn't happening much these days. And Robert? I didn't know what to think about Robert and his father. Yesterday Doyle had reached out and grabbed onto Robert like a drowning man. But today he'd gone and slapped Robert across the clubhouse.

I had to get one thing straight. "I can still go play with Baby and Robert, can't I?"

"Give it a couple of days," Mama advised. "Let's make sure Doyle's really staying away. I'd feel better knowing you weren't over there. But they can still come here to play."

"What about the clubhouse? Our collection?"

"It'll still be there. Once we see what's what, then we'll talk about it again. OK?"

"OK. I guess."

I got up, fetched my toast, slathered it with homemade strawberry jam, and sat back down. Everyone was quiet. I glanced around as I was chomping into my second big bite and saw that both Grandma and Mama were staring at that ugly white brassiere-thing on the table.

Mama cleared her throat and straightened her shoulders. "You haven't thanked Grandma for buying you this," she said.

I slid down farther into my chair so that my shoulders were barely above the level of the gray Formica tabletop. I took the biggest bite of toast I could and carefully avoided looking at either of them. "Thuumble...yuumble," I said, chewing hard.

Mama gave me that *You listen to me, young lady* look. "I said, 'You haven't *thanked* Grandma yet.'"

I sighed. There was just no sidestepping this one. "Thanks," I barely whispered, not looking at Grandma. And then, sitting up in my chair, I said louder, "But I'm not wearing it."

"*Jessssica*," Mama said.

"I'm not," I said to Mama. And then, to Grandma, "I'm just not. And that's a fact."

"Maybe not right away," said Mama. "But someday soon you'll need to."

I stretched out one finger and flicked the bra, sending it scooting across the table toward Grandma. She watched me, scowling.

"She isn't ever going to grow up into any kind of respectable woman, Mirabelle," said the Ol' Biddy. "She's run wild over these hills for so long she thinks she's a boy."

"Please, Mother," Mama said, "let's not start on that right now."

Well, Grandma had got my goat again, but after everything that had happened I was just about tuckered out. Besides, with Mama there I remembered my promise to count to ten. So I did.

When I was calmer, I said, helpfully and reasonably,

"Anyway, I don't see the point." I reached out and picked the bra up with two fingers so that it dangled between us. "I mean, look at it. It's flat. And I don't have a bosom anyway."

"Hmmph! I *did* want to get one that would fit," said Grandma.

I looked at Mama.

"You'll get used to wearing one if you start with this," she said.

"What's wrong with my undershirts?" I asked. It seemed like Grandma and Mama were ganging up to get me strapped into this...this contraption. I slumped way down in my chair.

I'd be the laughingstock of the whole school if anyone found out. It would look like I was having hopes of being something I wasn't. The boys would be sure to find out, and I'd be the target of a snap attack. The boys grab a girl's bra from behind and rear back and snap it really good. If you were DeeDee or Lorelei, you giggled, fake-like. But that just wasn't me. I'd punch anybody who did that to me.

I turned and leaned way over toward my mother so Grandma wouldn't hear and pleaded, *"I haven't got anything to hold up, Mama."*

"Honey, someday you will," she whispered back and reached over to push the hair out of my eyes. "Go on. Keep it in your drawer for right now," she said.

I slid from my chair, but before I started back to my room with the brassiere, I turned to Grandma. It took all the strength I had to say, "Thank you, Grandma."

seventeen

I WENT INTO HIRAM on my bike the next day. I wanted to thank Adam for getting us five dollars in exchange for the gift certificate. And I thought he might help me figure out how to raise another fifteen dollars.

There was a good-sized commotion going on in front of the First Farmers and Tenants Bank. Several cars were parked there, and folks were walking around with cameras and other kinds of equipment. I pedaled over and saw Adam in the crowd.

I stood up and straddled my bike. "What's going on?"

"Reporters," said Adam as he tousled my hair by way of a greeting. "Some photographers, too."

"How come? Has there been an accident?"

"No. I think they're here to cover the mine closing at Greasy Ridge."

"Oh," I said. "I thought the news had already covered that."

"Well, there've been developments—some violence up Greasy Ridge way. I guess a group of the miners were trying to reopen the mine themselves," Adam explained.

I watched for a bit, a little bored, as the town fathers, especially Mr. McMasters and Mr. Byrum, kept trying to hog the reporters' attention with their viewpoints on the situation. Then I saw Miss Woodruff talking to a couple of fellows with camera equipment by an old blue station wagon. I waved to her.

"Jessica! Jessica!" she called and gestured for me to come over.

"See you later," I told Adam.

"OK." He smiled. "Let me know if you find out anything more. And Jessie?"

"Huh?"

"I'm sorry we didn't get that prize you wanted to win in the raffle. Your mother would have liked it."

"That's OK," I said. I realized I had forgotten to thank him. "Thanks for bringing over the five dollars. I've got plans for that, too."

"Well, say howdy to Mirabelle for me. Tell her...uh... tell her I might stop by sometime soon to see how she's getting along. OK?"

Other than needing to relax a little, I thought Mama was getting along just fine. But it was all right with me if Adam stopped by. I shrugged and said, "Sure."

I made my way over to Miss Woodruff, walking my bike through the crowd. She introduced me to a reporter, a Mr. Gerald Birchfield, and a photographer, a Mr. Louis Henry, from New York City. I thought it was kind of funny that the photographer had a second first name and was using it as a last name.

"Are all these people here because of the miners?" I asked her.

"Some are," said Miss Woodruff. "But Mr. Birchfield and Mr. Henry are also planning on taking some pictures and reporting on the work we're doing around Hiram and Baylor for the War on Poverty. They'll be documenting how our federal dollars are helping the poor. Maybe their reporting will also help us get more funding."

Mr. Birchfield smiled. "Yeah, we'll be taking some local color shots and interviewing some of the citizens."

"What are 'local color shots'?" I asked.

"Oh, pictures of the local people doing what they do every day, or interesting local things that the rest of the world might want to know about."

It looked like the interview with the city fathers about the mine closing was finished. Mr. Henry loaded up several cameras into a huge bag. The rest of the out-of-town folk were all packing up to leave.

Suddenly, I had an idea about that other fifteen dollars.

Photographers wanted pictures of local color. And Lester had said that sometimes photographers paid people to let them take their picture. So why couldn't they take my picture? Heck! I'd let them do that for fifteen dollars—even five dollars—and they could take several.

Maybe if my picture got printed in the paper, we could put it up in the clubhouse. I smiled to myself. That would be nice—to be up on the wall with all the movie stars.

Mr. Henry had put most of his gear into the station wagon, and everyone was just about ready to leave. When

Mr. Birchfield and Mr. Henry walked back our way to say goodbye, I figured it was now or never. "Um, I know where you can take lots of interesting local photographs."

"You do?" asked Mr. Henry.

"Sure. Uh, local color. My friend Robert and I have a clubhouse with pictures of movie stars all over the walls. And..."

"Jessie, I'm not sure they're interested in that sort of thing," said Miss Woodruff.

"OK, then." I was clutching my bicycle and trying desperately to think of something local that was interesting. What had I shown Miss Woodruff that was special? "How about Crazy Cooch?"

"Crazy Cooch?" asked Mr. Birchfield. "Who's that?"

"He's a dog, and he stands on his head. That's local color, isn't it?"

"What!" Mr. Birchfield was laughing. "You're kidding us now, young lady."

Miss Woodruff shook her head and laughed, too. "No, it's true," she said. "I would never have believed it myself without seeing it." She turned to me. "Are you sure Miss Maybee won't mind newspaper people coming to see Cooch?"

"No, no. It'll be all right," I said, crossing my fingers. "I'll take you there to see for yourself."

They chuckled. "OK," said Mr. Birchfield. "We're going to be in town, anyway. We'll come around tomorrow morning to see this dog that stands on his head."

"Where do you live?" asked Mr. Henry.

"In Baylor, about two miles straight thataway," I said, and

pointed back over my shoulder. "Number 208. There's only one real road."

"Thanks." Mr. Henry stood there looking at me quietly for a moment or two. "You know, we could use a local guide, somebody who knows everybody," he said.

"I know almost everybody hereabouts. I could be your guide. Ask Miss Woodruff. She can tell you. I did a good job for her. I'd do a really good job for you."

"That's true," Miss Woodruff said. "Jessie knows almost everybody, and everybody knows her. You couldn't ask for a better guide."

"But," I went on, screwing up my courage, "it'll cost you five dollars."

"*Five dollars!*" Both men turned to look at Miss Woodruff.

"I know it's a lot," I said quickly. "But I'm the best guide you could get, and anyway, the money's going to a good cause. A special cause," I said, nodding at Miss Woodruff, who had her hand over her mouth. I knew she was trying to stop another laugh from coming out.

Then I shut up and looked from one of them to the other, holding my breath and clutching the blue rubber grips on my handlebars so tight that my knuckles turned white.

"Okay," said Mr. Henry. "We'll take that deal. We'll go see this dog that stands on its head, you'll introduce us around, and you promise to be the *very best guide* we could get."

"The very best," I promised, and raised my hand to put it over my heart.

Miss Woodruff burst out laughing, pushed her glasses up, and winked at me.

eighteen

THE NEXT DAY, WHEN Mr. Henry and Mr. Birchfield showed up at my house, Mr. Henry gave me the five dollars for my wages right up front. I ran inside and put it in my Smokey Bear bank, and then back out to do the job I'd contracted to do. I'd told Miss Maybee that Mr. Henry and Mr. Birchfield were trying to get some pictures of exceptional local happenings and that since Cooch was so exceptional, he'd fit right in. So she'd said it was OK to go over and see Cooch.

Unfortunately, Cooch was not in a very cooperative mood when I took Mr. Birchfield and Mr. Henry over there. We all stared at him lying stretched out in a patch of morning sun on Miss Maybee's dirt driveway, yawning.

"C'mon, Cooch. C'mon, show them what you can do," I pleaded, slapping the sides of my legs. All Cooch did was blink.

I heard Mr. Henry clear his throat.

"C'mon, Cooch!" I shouted and snapped my fingers in the air over his head. I hoped to get him on his feet, at least—then maybe it'd come to him that he really wanted to stand on his head. But it wasn't any use. Even when I gave him a gentle poke, he just looked at me and scratched behind his ear with his hind leg.

"He *does* do it," I told them. "Maybe we should come back later. It's hard to tell when he's going to be in the right mood." I saw Mr. Henry raise an eyebrow at Mr. Birchfield.

I showed them around what there was to see of Baylor, the way I had Miss Woodruff, and they snapped a few pictures. Then they wanted to go up a couple of the hollers to see if folks would let them take some pictures up there. I got permission from Mama first, and then the three of us got into Mr. Henry's station wagon with a whole lot of camera equipment. We headed up Dog Gap Holler, where the Whittens, the Applebys, and the Purchells lived.

Dog Gap's a hard place to drive a car through. The road is dirt that's topped with brittle red cinders, and some of the lanes to the houses are almost straight uphill.

We went up near the head of Dog Gap and worked our way back down toward Baylor, stopping at the Applebys' house, where Mr. Henry took some pictures of Mr. Appleby on his front porch and proudly standing by his pickup truck. Nobody was home at the Purchells' house. Then we stopped at the old lane that led to the Whitten place. Mr. Henry took one look at the lane where it forded Martin's Creek and decided it was too rocky to take his car up.

I told Mr. Henry and Mr. Birchfield that it was a good thing we weren't stopping by the Whittens' because Dickie and I always seemed to end up in a fight whenever we saw each other. And besides, I told them, Mr. Whitten supposedly had a whiskey still on the side of the mountain behind his barn, so it wasn't safe to go taking strangers up there. Mr. Henry and Mr. Birchfield agreed, especially when I told them that Mr. Whitten also liked rattlesnakes and kept a few pet ones around.

So in a little bit we came back down Dog Gap and started up Rockcastle to where the Weavers lived. When we got there, Mrs. Weaver came out on the porch with two or three of her youngest ones hanging off her.

"Miz Woodruff ain't to home right now," she said, wiping her hands on a raggedy dishrag. "She be in Bartlettsville. Expect her tereckly."

I introduced Mr. Henry and Mr. Birchfield and told Mrs. Weaver that they were here to visit with her. So she stayed on the porch to chat with them. Mr. Birchfield took some notes, and Mr. Henry took some pictures of her and the kids. Mrs. Weaver would have been pretty, I thought, if she wasn't so worn out–looking. Her faded housedress was held together at the top with a couple of safety pins. Her limp hair kept falling down into her eyes as she grappled with first one little one and then another, who were intent on investigating Mr. Henry's camera and camera cases.

Sitting on a stump back a ways by where we'd parked the car, I had attracted an audience myself. One of the littlest Weavers—I couldn't remember whether it was a boy or a girl—came toddling down the path with a dripping-wet diaper and sat down, right on my sneaker. "Hey!" I yelled, and slipped my foot out from under its wet bottom.

Then Clay Weaver came over and stood watching me. He was about seven. He didn't say a word for the longest time. Finally, he pointed at me and asked if I owned a tooth-brush. "Of course," I answered him, wondering why in the world he'd want to know that.

"Yup," he said, nodding his head. "I figured as much. Miz Woodruff, she got her a purty blue one."

"So?" I asked.

"So I aim to get me one, one of these days. Yes, sir." He said it like it was the most important thing in the world.

I started to laugh, and then something made me shut my mouth. I looked past him and saw that Mr. Henry had reached round to his back pocket and pulled out some money to give to Mrs. Weaver. I was glad of that.

After visiting the Weavers, I hoped to get Mr. Henry and Mr. Birchfield over to the clubhouse to take some pictures. I figured Mama wouldn't mind because even if Doyle turned up, I'd be safe with the two of them. Maybe they'd take my picture, too. But first we swung by Miss Maybee's again to see what Cooch was doing.

When we pulled into the driveway, there he was, stand-ing on his head as pretty as you please.

"See there?" I said, jumping out of the car as Mr. Henry hurried to get his cameras. "What'd I tell you? Did you ever know a dog to do that in New York City?"

"No, I have to admit this is the first time I've ever seen anything like this," Mr. Birchfield said. "Do you have any idea why he does it?"

"Nope. Just does," I said, and grinned. "Miss Maybee

thinks he does it only when there's been some animal around. But I've seen him just get up from a nap and do it. Dr. Meyer, the vet over in Bartlettsville, says he's really just standing on his front paws and resting his head on the ground, that his head isn't taking the weight." We all kind of tilted our heads sideways and stared at Cooch's short little legs, his thick, short body, and his flat head.

"What kind of dog is he?" asked Mr. Henry.

"Just a mutt. My friend Lester says he's got Bluegrass Bandy-legged Bantam in him."

"A bantam's a chicken, isn't it?"

"That's just what Lester says. Cooch showed up in front of Miss Maybee's one day and stood on his head. So she fed him and he stayed. I guess he liked Baylor."

"Hmm." Mr. Birchfield pulled out his notepad and headed up to Miss Maybee's house while Mr. Henry took some snapshots of Cooch from all kinds of angles. I went up on the porch with Mr. Birchfield.

We knocked and waited a few minutes but nobody came. We were just turning around to go back down the steps when Baby walked out the front door with a peach in one hand and a cookie in the other. "Hi, Jessie. Miss Maybee's gone," he said.

"Thanks, Baby. We'll take you home, OK?" I offered. "We're headed over that way...to the clubhouse." I'd just stepped off the porch to lead the way when Mr. Birchfield stopped me.

"Who's this?" he asked.

"Oh, this is Baby Blue. He just stopped in to get some-thing to eat."

105

"Baby Blue?"

"Well, his real name's Morton Ketchum, but he doesn't go by that," I told him.

"What's he doing here all by himself?"

"'Grazing' is what some folks say," I said. "When he's hungry, he just stops in somebody's house to eat. It's OK. The people around here don't mind." I took Baby by the wrist and started across Miss Maybee's yard. "I've got one more place to take you," I said over my shoulder. "You'll really like it."

"Wait a second," Mr. Henry said. Now they were both studying Baby.

The peach juice had dripped down onto his bare chest. He was barefoot, and today he was dressed in a pair of ripped shorts that were twisted way over to one side. Overall he was pretty dirty and sticky-looking, even for Baby. He must have slipped past Beryl Ann and Robert before they'd gotten a good look at him. I was pretty sure Robert was searching for him right now.

"I think we've found what we're looking for," Mr. Henry said.

nineteen

MR. HENRY KNELT DOWN and took a few quick shots of Baby, even waiting as he opened Miss Maybee's door, went back in, and got himself another cookie. All the while, Mr. Birchfield tried to get some words out of Baby. I'd already warned them that he didn't talk much.

Mr. Birchfield asked Baby where his father was. "He's gone," Baby said.

"And where's your mother?" asked Mr. Birchfield. Baby shrugged.

"You can probably find her at the Piggly Wiggly," I muttered as I sat on the porch step with my chin in my hand.

That was about all they could get out of Baby. When he'd finished his second cookie, he walked over to Cooch, who was right-side-around now, and lay down in the dirt with the last of his peach. He put his head on Cooch's freckled belly.

I was getting awfully impatient. I'd wanted to show Mr. Henry and Mr. Birchfield the clubhouse all day and here was Baby taking up their time. Besides, I was starting to feel a little funny about them taking pictures of Baby without asking Beryl Ann if it was OK. I wondered if they were going to offer Baby some money, too. I thought it might be OK then, because the Ketchums could use the money.

Finally, I'd had enough. While they took pictures of Baby napping with his head on Cooch's belly, I came over to them and said, "He's just sleepy now, that's all. He does this all the time when he's hungry; it's no big deal. Folks don't mind; sometimes they even leave food out for him."

"That's the point," said Mr. Birchfield. Then he smiled at Baby Blue covered in cookie crumbs, as he and Cooch lay together in the dirt.

The point? I thought. *What point?* After all, Baby was just being Baby. They didn't seem to understand. Oh, well. I wasn't going to waste any more time trying to explain it.

I leaned over and pulled Baby up by his hand. "Wake up," I whispered in his ear. "Robert's probably looking all over for you." I got him upright and tried to dust him off a bit. I waited a minute or two, holding Baby's hand and hoping Mr. Henry or Mr. Birchfield would think to offer him some money. When none appeared, I trotted him home across the road. Then I hurried back to Miss Maybee's.

Mr. Henry and Mr. Birchfield were loading up their equipment. "So now you want to go over and see the clubhouse? We've got lots of pictures of movie stars."

"You don't say!" said Mr. Henry.

"Actually, kid," said Mr. Birchfield as he put away his notepad, "it's been a pretty full day and I think we've got about everything we need now. You've been very helpful."

"I have?"

"Sure," said Mr. Birchfield. "We have some good stuff here: Mrs. Weaver and her kids, that little boy, and even the dog."

"Maybe next time we'll see your clubhouse," said Mr. Henry. "We'll be here another day working with Miss Woodruff, and then we may come back in a week or so to do some follow-up work. But look, here's some more money for thinking of the dog, and for that little boy, too. Here's five more dollars for the day. It's been worth it. I think we've got some good shots, and if we need to do anything more, that'll guarantee that you'll show us around again. OK?"

I was speechless. In my hand sat five one-dollar bills! I just stared at those five dollars with my mouth open.

"So long, Jessie," said Mr. Henry as he waved and got in the car.

"'Bye, kid. And thanks," said Mr. Birchfield.

"See you," I said. Cooch had staggered up onto four feet. We watched them drive away.

I looked at the money in my hand again and knelt down and gave Crazy Cooch the biggest hug I could. "Ten dollars, Cooch! This five and the five dollars they gave me earlier— that makes ten dollars in one day!"

I was so excited I kissed Cooch on his brown cheek. He looked at me, stretched one hind leg out behind him, walked away a couple of feet, went around in a bunch of circles, and promptly stood on his head again.

"Oh, Cooch!" I said happily. "You're one crazy dog."

Then I remembered what Mr. Henry said. This money

was "for that little boy, too." I was supposed to split it with Baby Blue. That was OK. I'd made a lot of money in one day, anyway. I turned and took off leaping through the field between our house and Miss Maybee's.

Back in my room I counted the money: sixty-seven cents from my bank, five dollars from the raffle, five dollars from this morning. And now I could add some more from the second five dollars Mr. Henry and Mr. Birchfield had given me. If I kept $2.50 of it, I'd have $13.17 and be $6.83 short of the twenty dollars I needed. But if I kept all of it, I'd have $15.67 and be just $4.33 short. Then I could pay for our part of Robert's glasses sooner.

I studied the five dollars that Mr. Henry had given me. I thought about Beryl Ann never having enough money saved up to get Robert a bike, even an old used one. I thought about Robert's glasses flying off when Doyle hit him. That's when I decided not to tell Beryl Ann about the money the photographers had given me. If I gave it to her, who knows how it might get used? And then Robert might still end up waiting months to get his glasses. Or Doyle might try to take it. No, the money would be much safer here in my bank.

I couldn't wait to tell Miss Woodruff how far along I'd gotten with the challenge. The whole rest of the day I could hardly keep my feet on the ground, and I couldn't stop whistling and singing to myself.

At suppertime Mama hugged me and said I was the light of her life. "No," I said. "*You're* the light of *my* life." Then I kissed her on the forehead this time.

"Jessica Kay, are you up to something?" Mama asked.

I just smiled and offered to wash the dinner dishes. I thought Mama was going to faint clear away. She cocked her head and stared at me. "You better be staying out of trouble, young lady."

"Mama," I said. "I'm working on something really good. You'll see. And I haven't been in a fight, or an argument in ... in ages. Anyway, at least since Grandma was here."

"OK." She looked at me doubtfully, yawned, and wandered into the living room to put her feet up.

I started on the dishes, smiling and imagining Mama so proud of me. I imagined my father, too, a respected doctor. His face was still a blur, but I was certain he would have green eyes and be as proud of me as I would be of him.

I blew the biggest bubble off the top of the sudsy water in the sink and watched as it floated away.

twenty

THE NEXT FEW DAYS flew by as I worked hard to earn the rest of the money. Lester usually paid me twenty cents a day to help out at the store while he or Mama was at lunch or running an errand. Sometimes I rang customers up. Sometimes I helped stock the shelves. It was also my job to count all the postage stamps when they came in. At twenty cents a day, I figured out that I only had to work twenty-two days to have $4.40. That'd be it! I wouldn't have to ask the Ol' Biddy, and I'd even have a few cents left over. School started in about five weeks, so the timing couldn't have been better.

One afternoon I was watching the store and baby-sitting Baby at the same time while Robert helped Beryl Ann with some canning. Baby was behind the counter by me, sitting on an upturned lard bucket and playing with a little garter snake he'd found out behind the store. If he wasn't hungry and didn't wander off, Baby Blue usually wasn't too hard to baby-sit.

Anyway, who should walk into the Gas & Go that day but Dickie and his daddy and a couple of Dickie's no-account friends from school, Bobby DeLong and Cy Meeks.

I clamped my teeth together, smiled, and determined to be as friendly and professional as possible, just like Lester.

"May I help you?" I asked.

"Whoa!" Bobby whistled. "Look who's here."

"It's Baby Ree-tard and your girlfriend, Dickie," Cy added.

I just couldn't find it in me to even get to the count of three. I started around the counter, but Dickie cut me off. "Shut up, you two," he grumbled.

"Isn't she the one that split your lip?" Bobby asked.

Mr. Whitten had gone right over to the automotive supplies, but now he turned back. "What's that?" he asked. Holding a can of motor oil, he walked back toward the counter. "I thought you fell off your bike. Your mama never told me no different."

Dickie's friends suddenly got quiet and awfully interested in the Joy bread sitting on the shelf nearby. "Aw, they don't know what they're talking about," mumbled Dickie.

"Speak up, boy! I'm talking to you," ordered Dickie's father, setting the oil down on the counter in front of me. "What's this about your split lip?"

"They got it all wrong," said Dickie, a bit louder.

"Do they now?" Mr. Whitten asked.

"Yes, sir."

"Well, then, why don't you straighten it out for me." Mr. Whitten crossed his arms and leaned against the counter, like he had all the time in the world. I could see a dark purple vein in the side of his neck jumping and throbbing. And I could tell that Dickie was squirming in his shoes.

One part of me was pleased to see Dickie getting what was due him. It served him right for being so mean all the time. But another part of me remembered what Adam had said about not wishing Mr. Whitten on any child as a father. And I remembered that sometimes Dickie came to school with bruises on him, and not just the ones I'd given him. I knew there were whispers about Dickie's mama, too, about her not coming to church for a spell. And one time she had lurched into the Gas & Go with dark glasses on and a swollen lip.

Watching that vein in Mr. Whitten's neck, I started to feel sick to my stomach. I didn't want to be part of this, but I couldn't leave the cash register or Baby. "Oh, it's OK, Mr. Whitten," I blurted out hopefully. "Dickie and I are friends. It was an accident, that's all."

Mr. Whitten slowly turned and looked at me. His eyes were the coldest eyes I'd ever seen. They just stared right down through me like they could see everything, even my lungs pumping in and out, faster and faster.

"You don't say?" he said.

"I'm sorry about that. I..." I let my voice trail off uselessly and shrank farther back behind the counter. Now I knew why Dickie was squirming. His father scared me so much I could hardly open my mouth.

Mr. Whitten looked back at Dickie. Then he took a red bandanna out of his pocket and rubbed his neck and face with it. "A split lip?" he asked. "From a *girl*, Dickie?"

"We...uh, we were just playing," Dickie said. He looked like one of those barn kittens that Miss Maybee found up in her loft last year; like he was just backing up and backing up, too scared to let anyone get near him. I was afraid he'd start crying any minute now.

I tried to think of something to stop it—anything. "That'll be seventeen cents!" I announced.

Mr. Whitten swung back to face me, faster than a snake. "What's that, girl?"

"I said, that'll be seventeen cents for the oil, sir, if that's all you'll be needing today." I didn't wait for Mr. Whitten to answer. I didn't even look up at him. I hit the cash register with my finger, concentrating so hard on the keys that I could hardly see the rest of the room around me. *Please*, I prayed, *please just pay for the oil and go.*

I snuck a look at Dickie while his father took out a cracked leather coin purse. A dark rage had replaced the pain across Dickie's face. And it was directed at me!

Mr. Whitten finished counting out his coins, snatched up the oil, and turned to leave. "You boys get going. You can walk to the river from here," he told Bobby and Cy. "Dickie's not going swimming after all. We've got some things to attend to at home." Bobby and Cy ran out empty-handed.

"C'mon," Mr. Whitten said. He held the door open for Dickie to march out. As he turned to leave, Mr. Whitten asked, "You Mirabelle Bovey's girl?"

I nodded my head yes, wondering why he wanted to know that.

He studied me a moment, then jerked his head toward Baby. "Likes snakes, does he?"

Before I could answer, he was gone.

I sank down on the floor behind the counter, next to Baby Blue. I was shaking all over. I knew Dickie was in for it when he got home, and I hadn't helped one bit. I even felt a little sorry for him.

Baby had the garter snake curled up in his lap. He stroked it gently with one finger down one of its little stripes. Baby looked at me. "It's OK now?" he asked.

"Yes. Yeah...it's OK." I sighed. But I knew it wasn't.

twenty-one

WHEN LESTER GOT BACK to the store, he paid me the twenty cents he owed me. I looked at those two dimes and thought, *This is an awfully hard way to make a living.* I was still shaking. Lester looked at me kind of funny-like and asked me if I was feeling all right. I was too sick to my stomach right then to tell him what had happened.

I walked Baby Blue back to his yard and watched as he went up to the house. The run-in with the Whittens had worn me out, and I just wanted to go home.

When I got there, I brought Mr. Perkins out to the living room, and we curled up together on the couch. We started watching this great monster movie about a man who gets attacked by some kind of frozen vegetable. I could tell Mr. Perkins wasn't too impressed, because he fell asleep pretty early on.

Anyway, I suddenly realized that Mama was talking with somebody at the kitchen door. I was a little surprised, because I hadn't even heard a knock.

I put Mr. Perkins down on the couch and got up and

backed out of the living room, trying to keep my eyes on the TV set. I didn't want to miss anything, but I wanted to know who had come. Quickly I peeked toward the kitchen door and almost fell over.

Mama was hugging a tall black man!

White people just didn't do that around here. Almost all the Negroes in Beulah County lived over across the river from Bartlettsville, in Ramsey. And although Mama had a few black friends, I'd never known her to clutch on and hug them the way she was hugging this stranger.

I was so surprised I must have made some kind of noise, because Mama let go of the man and turned to me. "Oh, Jessie! Jessie! I'm so happy. Look who's come for a visit!" she cried.

The visitor was an elderly man with a little gray at his temples. He was dressed well, better than I'd ever seen a black person dressed unless they were on *The Ed Sullivan Show* or going to Sunday meeting at the Sanctified Church in Ramsey.

Mama put her hand behind my back and gave me a little shove forward, like she wanted to show me off. I didn't know who the man was or what Mama expected of me.

In the back of my mind Grandma's voice popped up. "You never know who you might run into." I hadn't cleaned up much, and cuddling in front of the TV with Mr. Perkins hadn't helped. I pushed a strand of hair behind my ear and wished I had some shoes on. I could plainly see that my feet weren't going to be listed in anybody's record book for cleanliness.

I tried to make the best of it. I smiled and put my hand out. "Howdy," I said. "I'm Jessie Bovey."

"Hello," the stranger said in a friendly voice. "We finally meet. I've been looking forward to this day for a long time."

Instantly, I liked him. But I sure couldn't think of anyone, let alone a Negro, who had been waiting to meet me. I turned to look at Mama over my shoulder and raised my eyebrows at her. *Now what?*

"Jessie," she said, "I'd like you to meet my old friend, Dr. Warren Harrison."

Well! All I could do was stare. I'm sure Mama thought I'd been struck stupid. She had to ask me twice to get some lemonade for our guest and bring it into the living room.

I opened the refrigerator, reached in, and stood staring at my hands and arms. All I could see was my white skin, a bit tanned and dirty but still very white. White and freckled. Certainly not black, or even brown. I couldn't move. I simply stood there, turning my hands and arms over and over in the light from the refrigerator.

I heard Mama call me. Did she know about the letter? What if he told her now? I turned my head slightly and looked at the screen door. I wanted to run out and hide under a rock.

Mama called from the living room again. "Jessica! What's keeping you?"

Then I heard Dr. Harrison say, "I'll go help her."

My heart was beating fast. I studied the screen door again, but I still couldn't move. It felt like my feet had grown roots that went straight down through the floorboards into the dark dirt underneath.

Then I heard his deep voice coming from just behind my shoulder. He had pulled up a kitchen chair next to me. Somehow he knew exactly what to do and say. "It's OK, Jessie," he whispered. "I won't tell your mother about the letter." Then, very gently, he leaned into the refrigerator and helped me lower my arms. He lifted out the pitcher of lemonade and stood to put it on the kitchen counter. I looked at him, unable to utter a word. My eyes started to water up.

"Get some glasses, and we'll talk while I pour," he said. Then he said back over his shoulder, toward the living room, "We'll be there in a minute, Mirabelle. I'm just helping Jessie get down some glasses.

"The letter is our secret," he whispered. "I had to come for a visit, though." I watched as he poured lemonade into our three best glasses. "Got any ice?" he asked.

Suddenly, I could move. I got the ice. I ran to get napkins and Mama's serving tray.

Finally, I stood still and looked up at him, able to speak again. "I'm sorry I bothered you; that you came all this way for nothing. You're not my daddy."

"Don't be sorry," he said. "I didn't come 'for nothing.' You're a brave girl, with one of the best mothers in the world. I had to come and meet you. I didn't want to send a letter— I was afraid Mirabelle would see it."

Somehow I hadn't thought of that!

"So," he continued, "forgive me for surprising you." Then

he did a wonderful thing. He took my hand, raised it, and kissed it, just like I'd seen gentlemen do on TV. "I've known your mother a long time and I've been waiting, it seems like forever, to make your acquaintance, Miss Jessica Kay Bovey. Even though I'm not your father, may I be your friend?"

"Yes," I whispered.

"Well, then," he said. He gave my chin a little shake with his hand as though he was trying to help me shake out any more tears that were threatening. "I think we better get back into the living room before your mother wonders what's going on."

"Yes." I nodded, took the tray, and led the way with my new friend.

In the living room Mama had tidied up a bit and was sitting at one end of the couch. I started to put the tray on the coffee table as Dr. Harrison bent to sit at the other end of the couch. I saw a little face peeking out from the cushions. "Mr. Perkins!" I yelled.

He stopped in mid-sit. "Mr. Perkins?"

"Between the cushions."

Dr. Harrison looked down and laughed. Before I could put the tray safely down and get Mr. Perkins, Dr. Harrison had rescued him from the couch.

"Jessie can—" Mama started to say.

"I don't mind," he said. He had Mr. Perkins cupped gently in his hands. "He's a great big specimen: *Bufo americanus,* American toad."

"Most people don't like toads," I said.

"I do," he said.

"You do?"

"Sure. I had all kinds of pets when I was a kid. I had toads, frogs, snakes—whatever I could catch or could entice to follow me home. I don't think my mother always appreciated it. If I hadn't become a doctor, I would have gone into veterinary science. Did you know that some toads like to have their backs scratched?"

"Mr. Perkins likes to be scratched right there!" I pointed to the spot.

Dr. Harrison sat down, put Mr. Perkins in his lap, and scratched him. "Oh, he does like that. Toads are interesting creatures, much more interesting than frogs, I think. They can actually be trained to come when you call them by name."

"They can?" I asked.

"Yes. And they live a lot longer than frogs, generally. In fact, I remember reading about one case of a toad that lived for thirty-four years under the porch of a house in England. He came out in the evening when called, to get his back scratched."

"No kidding?" I asked.

"No kidding," Dr. Harrison said, nodding.

Mama put her hands up. "Please! Don't tell me I'm going to be raising a toad all by myself when Jessie's old enough to go off to college."

"I'll take him to college with me," I said.

"Toads may be smart, but I doubt if they're that smart!" Mama joked. "Anyway, for right now, why don't we put Mr.

Perkins back in his terrarium? And you two toad lovers can go get all those toad germs washed off your hands before we have our lemonade."

"Mirabelle," Dr. Harrison said, "you would have made a good nurse."

"Hmm, I don't know about that," Mama said. "Go put Mr. Perkins away, Jessie."

"Here, I can take him," I said, retrieving Mr. Perkins and whispering to him, "You've got a new friend, too."

twenty-two

OUR FRIEND WARREN—he said I should call him that—stayed for dinner. He was on his way to a conference in Georgia and had left Chicago a day early to stop in and see us.

We used our holiday dishes and the store-bought tablecloth, and Mama beamed and gabbed all evening. After dinner we played rummy and I won. Warren accused me of being a card shark. "I bet your grandmother's been teaching you some of her tricks," he said.

"Grandma?" I asked blankly.

"Don't tell me she hasn't taught you some of the things she learned in Las Vegas?" Warren shook his head and laughed. "Now, *she's* a card shark."

This didn't surprise me. It figured that Grandma was a card shark. She was probably a sneaky one, too.

"Mirabelle told me in her letters that Anna Mae's lived in a lot of interesting places," he continued. "She's a fascinating woman."

"Grandma?" I asked again.

"Jessie and my mother haven't been...well, on the best of terms lately," Mama said.

"She doesn't like Mr. Perkins," I told Warren. "Among other things." I didn't want to spoil the night by going into the whole long list of what Grandma didn't like.

"Well, she's always been a woman of strong convictions. I admire her for that."

"Grandma?" I repeated.

Mama gave me a look, and then said to him, "We're working on Grandma."

Warren slowly dealt the next hand. "I see," he said. And then with a little arch of one eyebrow he asked, "So, what kind of car is she driving these days?" We all three looked at each other and cracked up laughing.

We were having so much fun that Mama let me stay up late. But even after I went to bed, I could still hear them talking quietly in the living room.

I was just drifting off to sleep when Warren came into my room. "I came to say goodbye," he said.

I sat up and turned on my seashell lamp. "You can come again. Anytime."

"I'll try." He smiled, and then he picked up my hand and held it for a moment. I looked at our two hands, one dark and one light.

"I'm so happy we've met," he said. "You weren't born yet when I left Hiram. I should have stopped by long ago."

"Why'd you leave?"

"Oh, lots of reasons," he said, shaking his head. "Mainly, it was time to go."

We were quiet for a while. I lay back down on my pillow wishing he could stay longer.

"Do you really think Mama would have made a good nurse?" I asked him.

"Absolutely! She was one of my best students. Has she mentioned nursing school lately?" he asked.

"No. I know she worked with you at the hospital and all, but now she works for Lester at the Gas and Go."

"How is Lester?"

"He says his joints hurt him. But Mama and I are taking good care of him."

"I bet you are," he said, smiling. "You know, Jessie, I don't have any children of my own. But if I did, I would want them to be as strong and as loving as you are."

"Hah!" I laughed. "Me? Loving? Mama says I fight waaaay too much. It's because I'm easily riled."

"That's only because you love so fiercely."

"You think so?" This was a totally new thought to me. I didn't know that love could be fierce.

"I'm sure of it. And I'm glad Mirabelle has you to love her so much. You hang on tight to each other," he said. Then he stood up to go. "I'll stop by again for another visit someday. And I'll give Mr. Perkins a good scratch then."

"You promise?"

"Promise," he said. Then he tucked me in, and was gone.

In the morning I thought he might have been a dream. But I knew he wasn't, because Mama was singing as she made biscuits and gravy for breakfast.

twenty-three

AFTER BREAKFAST MAMA SAID, "Come here, light of my life." She began to measure me for a new school dress. "You're growing so much I can't use one of your old dresses as a pattern. I'll have to make a new pattern from scratch." She always made her own patterns from pieces of newspaper rather than spend money buying them.

"Stand still!" she ordered, laughing. I tried not to fidget as she measured and jotted down numbers on a little scrap piece of paper.

I listened to her humming to herself and decided to take advantage of having almost all of her attention. "Mama?"

"Hmm?" she mumbled, the tape measure in her mouth. She pushed up on one arm, set my hips straight, and generally manhandled me into the position she wanted.

"I've never met a Negro doctor before."

"Well," she said, taking the tape measure out of her mouth and starting to stretch it down my arm, "there aren't many around here. But there are lots in Chicago, where he lives and works now."

"He said you were one of his best students."

"He did, huh? Well, he was one of my best teachers. There was a special program at the Hiram hospital back then for students to see if nursing or doctoring was something they really wanted to do. Warren was setting that program up. That's how we met."

I remembered that Grandma always snorted or shook her head whenever his name was mentioned. "And he's not just a teacher, he's a real doctor, too?"

"Yes!" Mama said, yanking my arm down.

"Ouch!"

"I'm sorry. He is *really* a doctor. And a good friend."

"How come he's such a good friend?" I asked. "You don't see each other much, not like Robert and me."

At this, Mama sat down at the table. She settled back into the chair and got quiet, like she was pulling thoughts in from a long, long way away. "He helped me once, through a very bad time. We helped each other. That's what friends do. And you don't forget that, no matter how far apart you live or how seldom you see each other."

I thought about how I was trying to help Robert get his glasses. "What bad time, Mama?" I asked.

Mama jotted down a number on her scrap paper, and sat staring at what she'd just written. She was quiet for so long that I was afraid to move.

"There was . . . there were some bad times for a little while around Hiram and Baylor. Believe me, the people here were not too happy about a black doctor coming to town — especially one who was supposed to take care of white patients and supervise white students and doctors in a new program. I think even the hospital was surprised when he got here." Mama looked at me and gave a little shrug. "Some people weren't too happy that we became friends."

"What happened?" I sat down on a chair by Mama. "Was that when..." I was almost afraid to ask it, but I'd heard bits of conversation all my life. "Was that when someone set fire to our house?"

Mama looked sharply at me. I ducked my head down and scratched at the tabletop. "Folks talk," I said.

"Yes. Unfortunately, they do." Mama took a deep breath and pushed aside her measuring tape, paper, and pencil. "I guess you're old enough to know some of this. And you've met Warren now.

"You see, some people didn't like it that Warren and I were friends. It might have been OK if he'd just been one of my instructors. But we ate lunch together, there in the hospital cafeteria or around town. And quite a few times he gave me a ride home. Grandma and I had the old Studebaker then. Half the time it didn't run. Your grandpa had been dead for a long time already, and he was the only one who'd been able to keep it going."

She sighed. "Certain people started calling me bad names. They didn't like seeing a white woman and a black man together. They were mean to Grandma and me, and, of course, very mean to Warren. Sometimes they played bad tricks on him. It got dangerous, for all of us."

"Adam says some folks are just plain mean, like Dickie Whitten," I said.

"Oh, Dickie. Well, Adam may be right. But sometimes

there's a reason for it. In Dickie's case, his father's a hard one. I wouldn't turn my back on Curtis Whitten, even in broad daylight."

After yesterday morning I knew exactly what Mama was talking about. "Was Mr. Whitten one of the people who was mean to you?"

"Yes. Him and others, too. Doyle wasn't very nice; he and Curtis would go out drinking together. Doyle tried not to show it too much, though, because Beryl Ann and I were such good friends.

"Anyway," Mama continued, "like I said, my daddy—your grandpa—wasn't there to help. Only Grandma and me in that little house. Lester tried to help. Warren, too, tried to make it not so hard on us. But we had to work together at the hospital. And you've met him; I couldn't help but like him. I know how much you liked your teacher last year, Mr. Prichard. Well, I liked Warren like that. And then, even though he was a lot older than me, we became friends the way you and Robert are. We always knew how to joke with each other, and how to help each other.

"Besides, I guess the famous Bovey temper runs in me, too. What right did anyone have to tell me who my friends could be? That just made me mad.

"Then one night, while Grandma and I were in Bartlettsville shopping, someone set the house on fire. Everything gone! All our family treasures, your great grandma's quilts, our pictures—gone. Though it wasn't much, that house had been your grandpa's pride and joy. It was hard on Grandma."

I'd always figured that the fire was why I'd never seen a picture of Grandpa Henry. I just hadn't been sure that the rumors were true—that someone had actually done it on purpose. But now I knew. Someone had come in the night and taken it all away: our house, our history, and our pictures of Grandpa Henry. I thought about Lester and his house, how right and permanent it felt, and I didn't have any of that. Someone had taken it all. "Who?" I asked, gripping the edge of the table. "Did they catch who did it?"

"No." Mama shook her head. "We tried to find out. The authorities said it probably burned down because it was old. But we knew the house was in good shape. No one believed Grandma when she told them. Actually, I don't think anyone wanted to know the truth. And then there were other things to worry about. We had to get on with our lives."

"What other things? Why didn't you fight them, Mama? Why didn't you make sure that whoever burned down our house got caught? I'd make them pay for it!" I said, folding my arms. I was furious. I couldn't understand why Mama hadn't fought back; I knew she wasn't a coward.

Mama pushed back her hair and looked at me steadily. "I was pregnant," she said. "You were on the way. That had to be our first consideration."

Suddenly, it felt like hot liquid was draining from my feet. Like someone had opened up a spigot on my heels and let all the anger out. "Oh."

"We needed money." Mama rushed on. "There were things we had to replace, things to buy for a new baby. There wasn't much insurance. Lester hired me to help him. And"—

she smiled—"you won't believe it, but Grandma even got a job in Bartlettsville.

"We lived with friends for a short time until our... until this house of Lester's became empty and he let us live here. It was hard on him, too, what with my pregnancy showing. People were talking about me; they didn't want me to wait on them in the store. But Lester, he stuck by us. Afterward, I just didn't have the energy or the time to go back to the student program at the hospital. Besides, Warren had left by then, and there were people at the hospital I did not want to work with anymore."

Mama fiddled with the stuff on the table. I didn't say anything for a long time. Finally, it seemed like the right moment to ask, "What about my father? Did he help us?"

Mama's head jerked up suddenly, and her mouth formed a tight line. "No. He didn't," she said.

Something wasn't right. The quick, hard look on Mama's face scared me a little. So instead I asked, "What about Warren? What did he do?"

"He helped us a lot. But he finally had to go. It got so he couldn't even see me for my checkups. People heard about it, they talked."

"What'd they say?"

Mama had relaxed a little again. She reached out, stroked my arm, and smiled. "Oh, mostly stuff to get other folks heated up. They didn't understand about my friendship with Warren, how we just liked to talk and make each other laugh. They said I'd have a black baby, for sure." She shrugged her shoulders again. "That part didn't bother me.

132

But after the house burned down, Warren said he had to leave, for my sake and for yours. *That* bothered me a lot! I cried a bucketful when he left."

Then Mama kind of shook me a little and looked into my face. "That's why he was so excited about seeing you yesterday. He went through a lot for you."

I'd thought he wanted to see me only because of my letter. "I like Warren. I wish he could have stayed longer," I said.

"Me, too." Mama smiled. Then she tapped me on the nose with her finger. "Just remember, there are lots of people who love you. And even if you can't be with them, they're still there, keeping a place in their hearts for you. Warren, Lester, Grandma—"

"Grandma?" I interrupted.

"Yes, *even* Grandma. I was so proud of her," Mama said. "She didn't let anyone talk down to me. Or to you, after you were born."

I couldn't picture Grandma standing up for me. "Are you sure?"

"Don't misjudge your grandmother," Mama warned. "Sure, she can be hard to get along with sometimes. But it's when things are bad and you really need to pull together that you judge a person. Grandma's been there for us when we needed her—always."

I still found this a little hard to believe and might have argued, but Mama stood up and said, "Well, we went to so much trouble to get you into the world, now let's get you measured so we can clothe you and send you to school."

"You could forget about the school part," I teased as she started measuring me around the chest.

"Now, let me see...a whopping thirty inches for the booooooooooozuums," Mama drawled out, making me crack up laughing. "But don't worry," she said. "Someday you'll leave DeeDee and Lorelei in the dust. Only yours will be real."

"Mama!" I said, shocked, as I thought, *Fat chance of that ever happening.*

We were laughing so hard that it was a complete surprise when Robert swung the screen door wide and stepped in. "Someone's wrecked the clubhouse!" he shouted and grabbed me by the hand.

twenty-four

THE CLUBHOUSE WAS A MESS. The pictures had been ripped off the walls and were scattered here and there. Some were torn, some were wadded up. Our cooler had been emptied and overturned, and the dictionary had pages ripped out. The chairs were on their sides and one had a broken leg. The single picture remaining on the wall—our only full-color glossy picture of the Beatles that Robert and I had sent away for—had been deliberately ripped down the middle. John and Ringo were on one side, and Paul and George on the other. Each half had been neatly put back onto a nail, like some final insult spit out at us.

I could hardly bring myself to take that last step from the dirt path across the threshold into the clubhouse. I stood for the longest time just staring at the wreckage inside. Who would do such a thing?

Mama and Beryl Ann were whispering to each other behind me. Mama had run almost as fast as I had.

Finally, Robert stepped inside, bent down, and started searching through the papers on the floor.

"What?" I whispered.

"My library book," said Robert, turning the cooler upright and closing the lid.

"And the logbook!" I said, rushing in.

I found the logbook in one corner, pages ripped out and crumpled. The whole list—the whole history of our collection—gone. Ruined! All that time spent working so hard on it, recording each picture, wasted now. I held up the tattered cover to show Mama and Beryl Ann. I saw Mama's jaw tighten.

Slowly I got up, walked out, and handed her what was left of the logbook for safekeeping. She bent over and hugged me. Then I turned and went back in to start cleaning up.

Robert and I took care of most of the mess, with a little help from Baby. Mama took the chair with the broken leg home to fix. Beryl Ann brought us a broom and some paper sacks to put everything into. When Beryl Ann hugged Robert, I thought she was going to be the one to break down crying.

We managed to save nine pictures that we could hang back up. Some of these were creased, and a few had a corner ripped or a hole gouged through them where they had been pulled off the nails. But they were the best we could find.

The cooler was fine. We kept the dictionary, though some of the pages would forever be missing. But we didn't find Robert's library book. It wasn't in the clubhouse or anywhere outside in the grass. Whoever had wrecked the clubhouse had taken it or thrown it away.

When we'd done what we could, we stood in the center

of the clubhouse and looked around. We'd put all the rescued pictures up on one wall. It didn't look the same. It wouldn't *ever* look the same to me.

Robert sat down on the cooler with his head in his hands. "I don't know what I'm gonna do about that library book," he said. "*Shackleton.*"

"Shackleton?"

"*Shackleton's Valiant Voyage.* I was only on Chapter Eight, too." He sighed. "I'll probably have to pay for it."

"Pay for it? Just tell Mrs. Peabody about the clubhouse." On top of everything else, I couldn't believe he'd have to pay for the book. "It wasn't your fault."

"Taking care of it was my responsibility."

"But you didn't know this was going to happen," I argued. Robert could be really thickheaded sometimes.

He shook his head at me and slumped farther down on the cooler.

I looked around again. Who could say that even this patched-up repair would last? Suppose someone came back to wreck the place again and again, until there wasn't anything left at all?

That was when I realized that something else had happened to us, something I, running free around Baylor all my life, hadn't even thought could be possible. Not until this minute had I ever felt unsafe here.

Mama had just told me about her bad times. But they seemed so distant, like history. It never occurred to me that anything could ever happen here, *now,* that would hurt us or change us.

I went up to one of the walls of the clubhouse and started pounding on it with my fist, over and over and over again. Robert didn't say a word.

When I was done, I leaned my forehead against the wall, shut my eyes, and just tried to stay right there—in one place in my mind. I wanted to stay where I could breathe deeply, where I hoped all the bad things had been pounded out and where there were only good things and good people remaining. But the bad people had a way of sneaking back in. Slowly I raised my eyes and looked at Robert, still sitting on the cooler.

"Dickie did this," I said. I was as sure of it as I am that my name is Jessica Kay Bovey.

"What?" asked Robert.

"I said, 'Dickie did this.'"

"How do you know?"

"He and his daddy were in the Gas and Go yesterday, with Bobby and Cy. I think I got him into trouble, but I didn't mean to."

Just then Mama and Beryl Ann appeared in the doorway. Mama had nailed a piece of wood onto the chair to replace the splintered leg.

"Do you want to go to the library, Robert?" asked Beryl Ann softly. "To talk to Mrs. Peabody about your book? Mirabelle said she'd drive us over, if you want. She doesn't need to go into work right away."

"Yes," said Robert. "I'd like to find out what I need to do."

I knew for sure that if anybody should pay for that book, it should be Dickie Whitten. But nobody was suggesting that we should find out who'd done this or see if we could get the book back. I stood in the cool darkness of the clubhouse watching Mama and Beryl Ann outside in the sunshine, framed by the dark wood of the doorway. Didn't they see it? Didn't they understand?

Mama raised a finger, pointed it at me, and said, "And *you* stay out of trouble while we're gone. Your grandmother's supposed to stop by in a little while. Keep an eye on Baby for a few minutes and go tell Lester that I'll be in later."

I nodded my head.

Mama studied me long and hard. "Did you hear me?" she asked.

"Yes'm."

And then they were gone.

I went to the door of the clubhouse and looked down at Baby sitting on the high worn doorstep. The strange thing was that I didn't feel steaming mad. That feeling had somehow vanished. I just felt sure of myself, and I knew what I had to do. I had to let Dickie know that he couldn't get away with what he'd done. We wanted that library book back.

I'd even try to say something helpful—if I could think of anything. Mama said to stay out of trouble. Surely, just talking reasonably to Dickie wouldn't get me into trouble.

"C'mon, Baby," I said. "We're gonna go pay a little visit to Dickie."

twenty-five

BABY AND I STOPPED by the Gas & Go and I gave Lester Mama's message.

As we were leaving, Miss Woodruff came in and wanted to chat. I was anxious to get over to the Whittens' before Mama got back or Grandma showed up, but we had to be polite.

Miss Woodruff was excited because a big national women's group was going to donate new school clothes for the miners' kids. The recent news programs on the mine closing had gotten the word out that some of the families needed help, and she'd been busy organizing it all.

Finally, when she'd purchased what she needed, I grabbed Baby by the hand and walked out the door with her.

"How's the challenge going?" she asked.

"Really good," I said.

"Great!" she said. "I've written to the regional office, but I haven't heard back from them. You haven't talked to Beryl Ann about it yet, have you? We probably shouldn't say anything to her until I get a response. Then I'll know what I can offer."

"Oh." I stopped walking and looked up at Miss Woodruff. "Miss Woodruff, when you do hear from your office, do you think you could *not* say anything to Beryl Ann or Robert?"

"Why not?"

"Because I'd like it to be a surprise. I've been saving up the challenge money all by myself, and I've almost got the whole twenty dollars. All I need is a little bit more."

Miss Woodruff tilted her head and smiled at me. "That's very kind of you, Jessie," she said. "And Mr. Henry and Mr. Birchfield will be back in town in a few days. It seems their work went so well the last time they were here that an article is coming out any day now in some of the very biggest newspapers. Thanks to you, in no small way. They want to do some more work in the area. And who knows—maybe they'll need a guide again."

I smiled back at Miss Woodruff. Maybe I could get the last of the money needed for Robert's glasses! "Let me know when they get here," I said. "Well, Baby and I have some things to do. Nice to see you again, Miss Woodruff." I started dragging Baby across the gas station lot.

"Do you need a ride?" she asked, pointing to her old green Pontiac by the gas pump.

"We were just headed up Dog Gap a little way," I said.

"That's still quite a walk. I can take you."

We got into the car and set off. While Miss Woodruff chatted with Baby up in the front seat, I sat in the back seat and stared out the window. I knew Mama might not like what I was doing. But I couldn't help it—I had to do it. I'd stay out of trouble; I'd be calm. The one thing I knew for certain was that I couldn't stand around and let somebody get away with hurting us again.

Miss Woodruff didn't want to take her car up the rocky two-track lane to the Whittens' house, so she dropped us off at the end of the drive on Dog Gap Road. "Are you sure this is OK?" she asked.

I nodded. "Thanks," I said, hurriedly getting Baby out of the car before Miss Woodruff could change her mind and take us back home instead. "We've been here lots." Which wasn't *exactly* true, but I had been with Lester a few times when he made a delivery of some supply or other to Mr. Whitten. "'Bye, Miss Woodruff." We waved as she drove off.

First we had to ford Martin's Creek, which was only about two inches deep and five feet wide. Baby splashed across the creek and waited for me on the other side. I started jumping across from rock to rock so I wouldn't have to take my shoes off. That's when I realized that Baby was still barefoot. Most of the time kids went barefoot around Baylor, but I probably should have made Baby put some shoes on.

The trees were thick on either side of us, and the rough track was difficult to walk. I stumbled against exposed bits of rock, thinking about how Mr. Whitten's old truck must rattle like the dickens going up and down here. No wonder he had bits of that truck tied on with baling twine and fence wire and it always looked like it'd fall apart if someone blew on it.

When we got out of the woods, we topped the hill we'd

been climbing and came to a flat area with a couple of old sheds and a corncrib on our left. I could see the road up Dog Gap clearly. No wonder the law could never seem to surprise Mr. Whitten and confiscate his moonshine makings. He could see them coming a long way off.

Mr. Whitten's patched-together truck was by the corncrib. Ahead was the house, old, unpainted, and up on stilts because it sat smack up against the mountain. To the right sat their barn, leaning way back toward the mountain, like it wanted to give up, lie down, and take a nap in the tall weeds that the Whittens hadn't bothered to mow.

Like a lot of the houses around here that have doors to open up to the breeze, the Whittens' house had two front doors. I took a deep breath and marched up the steps to knock on the closest door, hoping that Mr. or Mrs. Whitten wouldn't be the one to answer. If one of them did come to the door, I'd simply explain the situation and ask if they'd seen a library book around.

I tried to calm myself and decided to count, just to be on the safe side. I counted to ten, and then to twenty. I took some more deep breaths. Baby sat with his legs dangling over the edge of the porch and waited.

No answer. I knocked louder and wondered how far I was going to have to count before someone came. Still no answer. "Dang!" It didn't seem like anyone was at home. "Now what?" I turned to look at Baby. He was gone.

"Baby?" I called. "Baby Blue!" This was not a good time for Baby to go wandering off. I jumped down the steps and searched the clearing in front of the house. No Baby. I took off toward the barn. Perhaps Baby had heard some animal there or had headed to the back of the house to let himself inside.

At first I didn't see them. I called again, "Baby!" Then, from over by the side of the barn, I heard someone laughing.

Dickie and Baby were standing by a big wooden box that sat atop a stump alongside the barn. I didn't like the fact that Baby was all by himself so close to Dickie. "Baby," I called, "come here!"

He didn't move, and Dickie barely glanced at me. I wondered what was going on. Dickie giggled. It didn't sound right, and my heart began to race.

I started toward them. Dickie swung around and looked at me. "You better stay back where you are. I got Ol' One Eye in here." He laughed again, high and nervously.

Dickie liked to tell tall tales, but I knew it'd be just like him to do something stupid like mess around with his father's snakes. "What are you doing?" I asked, taking one or two steps closer and stopping.

Dickie's eyes were little slits as he smiled at me. "I was just asking Baby here how he'd like it if I tossed him in that box with Ol' One Eye."

"That's a mean thing to say, Dickie." I took another step in their direction. "Baby, you come over here by me!"

Baby acted as though he hadn't even heard me. He stepped closer to the box.

"That's right, Baby. You want to see the purty snake, don't you?" Dickie asked.

"Quit teasing him, Dickie!" I shouted.

"I'm not teasing," he said. "Folks say he's got a weirding way with animals, especially snakes. Even my daddy says so. I thought he'd like to see Ol' One Eye."

And then I saw that Dickie had a stick in his hands. He raised it, poked at the box, and flipped the lid open. At the same time he took a step back. Suddenly, I realized that Dickie wasn't fooling with us. Maybe his daddy's rattlesnake really *was* in there.

Baby leaned over, looking into the box.

I darted forward, planning to grab Baby, but that's when the box fell off the stump. It landed on its side, lid open, on the ground between Dickie and Baby.

Out of the box slithered the biggest rattlesnake I'd ever seen.

twenty-six

"DAMN!" I SAID OUT LOUD. I thought my heart was gonna bust right out of my chest and start running away all by itself while the rest of my body stood there and watched that muscular diamond-patterned back slide slowly out of the box. I could hardly drag my eyes off of Baby's bare toes — right in its path.

"Don't . . . don't move," I said.

I heard Dickie squeal, a little high, scared-sounding titter.

"Shut up, Dickie! Don't move, either of you. I'll . . . I'll . . ." What was I going to do?

I knew nobody was in the house, or Dickie wouldn't have gotten the snake out to begin with. Looking around wildly, I stumbled into the clearing in front of the house. I could see a white car just pulling onto Dog Gap Road down below. Help — that was what we needed! I'd get help.

I ran down the Whittens' rocky drive so fast I could barely see the trees and rocks blurring past me. I know I fell a few times, scraping my knees and sliding on the palms of my hands against the crumbly rock of the road. But I didn't feel it. I just jumped back up and kept running. At the bottom I splashed across Martin's Creek and headed out onto Dog Gap Road.

Hurry! Hurry, or it's going to be too late! I repeated over and over to myself as I gulped what breath I could with each step. *It'll be too late and Baby's gonna get bit and die. Baby's gonna die, and it'll all be my fault! My fault for dragging him here. My fault for being mad at Dickie.*

On Dog Gap Road I fell down again in the loose gravel. My hands and knees were all bloody. But I got up and ran on. Only now I was crying, too. Where was that car? I'd just seen it. Had it passed by already?

How long, I wondered, before the rattler sniffed them out? How long before one of them got bit? I knew the stories of snakebites, of kids dying, a leg or arm swollen, black, and split open from the poison. "Oh, God! Oh, God!" I began crying out loud as I staggered down the road.

I came around a curve, holding my hands against my hurting chest, and almost ran directly into the white car as it slammed on its brakes. Behind the wheel was Grandma.

"Jessica!" Grandma yelled as she flung open her door, jumped out, and grabbed me. "Jessica!"

I couldn't get my breath. I stared blurrily at Grandma and then pointed, with every bit of strength I had left, behind me. "Baby... Dickie... rattlesnake."

Grandma looked past me, up the road. Then she pushed me in through the driver's door. I stumbled in, my head banging first against the dashboard and then against the far door as she shoved the car into gear and floored the gas pedal. Gravel and cinders flew up all around us.

It took me a few moments to get my breath. I reached up, grabbed the dashboard, and dragged myself upright. I could see the blood from my hands and knees smeared all over Grandma's white upholstery.

"One of them bit?" she shouted above the sound of the engine and the flying gravel.

"Not yet," I answered. I explained how Dickie had been trying to scare Baby and how Ol' One Eye's box had tipped over right at their feet. "And Baby's barefoot. I told them not to move, not to move one inch. Then I looked up and saw a car coming and ran down to get help. Grandma, it was crawling right toward Baby's feet!"

"You did good, Jessica!" Grandma said.

As she wrestled with the steering wheel, Grandma shouted about how Miss Woodruff had felt funny leaving us in Dog Gap. "It's a good thing I stopped in to see Lester! She'd just told him where she'd dropped you two off!"

I pointed to the Whittens' drive up ahead and tried to concentrate. The easiest thing for me to concentrate on was Grandma. She had on dangly earrings, and her black dyed hair was pulled back and held up with bobby pins. On the floor next to her sat her old leopard-skin purse. I looked down at her feet. She had on tiny little strappy yellow sandals. How would she get up that old lane? She couldn't run uphill in those.

I had my answer soon. Grandma barely slowed down as she careened onto that two-tracker. And then she splashed the car right across the creek, banging off rocks and jumping the Thunderbird this way and that.

A rock outcropping made the car tilt scarily sideways—we were up on two wheels. Grandma maneuvered the Thunderbird and it bounced as it slipped down again—*thunk!*

"That Curtis!" complained Grandma over the racket the car was making. "A two-year-old could build a better road than this with his eyes closed!" And then she let loose with a string of cuss words that made me sure God was going to strike us down before we even got there.

I didn't wonder what Grandma was going to do until we were almost to the house. Then I remembered she was scared to death of snakes. I asked myself if I should've kept on running to the Stanley farm, out on the main road. Maybe I should have made Grandma get Mr. Purchell to come back with us. But I hadn't thought of it.

Then we were in the clearing, and Grandma jumped out of the car. We took off past the house, me flat-out fast in my sneakers and Grandma bringing up the rear in her little yellow sandals. Now I was starting to get really worried. What the heck could Grandma do?

At the barn we stopped, and I bent over and tried to get my breath back. When I raised my eyes, the first thing I saw was Ol' One Eye curled up a few inches from Baby's bare toes.

Baby was singing a little song to himself. I could barely hear it. All the time he was singing he kept his eyes down and slightly away from the snake. It was almost like Baby was singing in his sleep. The snake had curled up as though it was trying to hear what Baby was singing.

Dickie was about two feet away from the snake and as stiff as a fence post. I saw him flick his eyes nervously over toward us. I could just feel what was going through his mind. Maybe he could jump back. Maybe, if the snake did strike, it would go for Baby instead of him.

I saw Grandma take the scene in. She turned away for a moment, as if she was going to be sick. Then she turned back and said loud enough for Dickie to hear, "You so much as flick an eyelash, Dickie Whitten, and I'll skin you alive before I feed you to that snake!"

Grandma turned on her heel and walked through the Whittens' back door without knocking. A minute or two later she came out again. In her hands was a .22 rifle.

twenty-seven

MY MOUTH DROPPED OPEN, but I didn't say a word. Grandma flipped her sunglasses up on top of her head and got a little bit in front of me. Then she hiked up her skirt, knelt down, and raised the .22 to her shoulder.

When I looked at Dickie, he seemed more scared than ever. I'm sure he was wondering, *What if she misses and startles the snake? What if she doesn't miss, and my daddy's favorite snake gets killed?*

I didn't know if Grandma could shoot or not, but I thought that Dickie was on the verge of bolting. "Don't move, Dickie," I said as loud as I dared to.

Grandma didn't take too much time, but I could tell she was getting a good line on that snake. I wondered how her stomach was feeling. I'd seen what happened when she'd caught sight of an itty-bitty garter snake slipping through the grass. I gulped and prayed for her to stay steady.

I saw the snake jump almost before I heard the crack of the rifle. Grandma rocked slightly from the kick the gun gave her. Then she brought it back to her shoulder, ready for a second shot. But it was obvious that Ol' One Eye was dead; part of him had gone flying through the air.

Dickie collapsed where he was and put his hands over his eyes. Even from where I was I could see him shaking and hear him crying.

Baby slowly turned and watched as Grandma strode over to them. Grandma glanced at Dickie. Then she looked at what was left of Ol' One Eye. A moment later she leaned against the barn wall with one hand and threw up.

I grabbed Baby by the shoulders and pulled him away. I'd heard about snakes that could still bite even after they were dead. Ol' One Eye's coils were easily three times the thickness of my arm. I didn't want Baby anywhere near that huge thing.

Baby and I waited while Grandma went to the Whittens' back porch to put the gun away. She opened up the chamber, shook the remaining bullets out, and gave it one last heft like she'd been handling rifles all her life before laying it down inside the back door.

Then I heard somebody crashing through the underbrush and charging down the mountain, and Mr. Whitten came rushing around the barn. "Hey! What...what's going on here?" he yelled. "Who's shooting?"

He came to a stop when he caught sight of Ol' One Eye's body on the ground beside Dickie. He looked at Dickie, and then at us. "Who shot my snake?"

That's when Dickie sprang to life and started scooting crab-like, trying to get as far away from his father as possible. "Dickie!" his daddy shouted. Dickie stopped suddenly, the tall weeds trembling above his head.

"She did," Dickie squeaked and pointed at Grandma as she came back to stand beside us. "She shot Ol' One Eye!"

Mr. Whitten swung around to glare at Grandma, like he was barely able to keep from exploding. I could feel her stiffen. She reached down and grabbed Baby Blue by one hand and tried to push me behind her with her other hand. The whole time, she never took her eyes off Mr. Whitten.

"For your information, I just saved your son's life!" Grandma snapped, lifting her chin. "Seems like you should be grateful."

"You," Mr. Whitten spat out, shaking his knotty finger at her. "You get off my property. Now! Or I won't be responsible for what happens."

"We were just leaving, *Mister* Whitten," Grandma said. She slowly turned us around, and we marched back to the Thunderbird. Mr. Whitten followed. I remembered what Mama had said about Dickie's daddy and I didn't like having my back to him, but I could tell Grandma was keeping an eye on him.

The once beautiful pure white Thunderbird looked like one of those cars from a demolition derby on TV. Long black scrapes covered both sides, except where the dents were too deep for the rocks and tree branches to have scraped across. The windows had crazy cracked patterns everywhere, and one of the headlights and a front fender had been smashed in.

Baby and I scrambled in through the driver's door and over to the other bucket seat. Grandma turned and stood just inside the open door. She reached down behind her with one hand and lifted her purse up off the floor of the car. The other hand was on the doorframe as she studied Mr. Whitten a couple of feet away.

"Any gentleman would thank me, Curtis," said Grandma.

Mr. Whitten looked like he wanted to jump out of his skin. He flailed his hands about in the air like he was searching for something to grab on to, or like he wanted to wring Grandma's neck. It was almost funny. And it was right then that I understood what Mama had been trying to tell me: no matter how mad you got, you had to learn to control it, to find a way to deal with it. Mr. Whitten had no control, and he was just plain ugly to look at.

Suddenly, he lunged at Grandma. "Oh! Oh!" I screamed, fumbling with the door handle on the passenger side. Mr. Whitten was a whole lot bigger than my tiny grandma. He'd throw her over his shoulder like a scrap of paper if he got his hands on her.

I was trying to scramble out of the car to help her when I heard a loud *whop!* Grandma had shoved the car door right into Mr. Whitten's middle with one hand and then swung around and walloped him up alongside his head with her leopard-skin purse.

"Keep an eye out for rocks, Jessica!" she shouted and jumped into the car before Mr. Whitten could get off the ground. She floored that Thunderbird, in reverse. We plowed up the ground in a big wide circle before she got it into forward and we took off.

Quickly I rolled my window down as we circled past him. I leaned out and yelled, "And make Dickie give back that library book he stole!"

We tore out of there like there was no tomorrow, bumping and jumping back down that drive. I couldn't help but have a big smile on my face. Yes, sir, my grandma was one tough old biddy. Boy, was I proud of her!

We rocked and tipped our way down from the Whittens' and forded Martin's Creek again before bursting out onto Dog Gap Road. Only then did anyone speak.

"I've got one thing to say to you, Jessica Kay," Grandma started.

Uh-oh. My smile disappeared. *Here it comes.* I knew I deserved every bit of what I was going to get for putting Baby's life in danger. I braced myself. "Yes, ma'am?"

Grandma looked quickly in her rearview mirror, smoothed her hair, and then grinned at me. "When you buy a purse, girl, invest in a damn good one."

twenty-eight

GRANDMA AND I SAT on the couch with our heads bowed and our hands in our laps as Mama paced back and forth, wearing a path in our green carpet and giving both of us what Lester calls "a frank talking-to."

Grandma tried to get a word in slantwise every so often, but she didn't have much success. I didn't dare open my mouth, other than to keep apologizing.

I could understand why Mama was angry with me. I had put Baby's life in danger, not to mention Dickie's. But I didn't understand why she was upset with Grandma, too. Grandma had saved the day. Leastways, that's how I looked at it.

Grandma tried to tell Mama about how I'd used my head, how I'd told them to not move, and how I'd gone for help right away when I'd seen somebody coming up the road. I could hardly believe it—Grandma was trying to stand up for me! Maybe that's why Mama was also giving Grandma a piece of her mind.

I kept my palms up and my knees out, hoping whenever Mama got a good look at the Mercurochrome and Band-Aids all over me she'd remember the good things I'd done.

But it didn't help much. We sat, Grandma and I, and listened.

The worst part came when Mama went on about how was she ever going to be able to trust me again. She kept throwing her hands up in the air and saying things like, "You *know* I have to work. I thought I could trust you. I *told* you to stay out of trouble. I just don't know what to do. I just don't know what to *do* with you.

"What am I supposed to do? Should I make you stay at the store with me, like I did when you were little? Should I get Araminta Boyd to check up on you all the time when I'm not here?" She stopped pacing and looked at me directly. "Jessie, I've got to trust you to do as you're told. It isn't going to work if you can't be trusted."

"Er...er," interrupted Grandma, raising her hand like she was in school. "Uh...I could stop by and stay with her, Mirabelle, till school starts up, if that's what you want."

I wasn't sure this was such a good idea. Though Grandma was my hero today, I knew how most of our run-ins ended.

"What I *want*," Mama said to Grandma, putting her hands on her hips, "is for her to act her age. She's going to be thirteen on her next birthday, for goodness sake! She's old enough that I shouldn't have to worry about her every time I turn my back. I thank God that Miss Woodruff let *some-body* know where they were."

I must have said I was sorry at least forty-seven-eleven times. I didn't know what else I could say in my defense. I could see now that facing down a rattlesnake just to get a library book back didn't seem highly reasonable. And I wasn't even sure we were ever going to see that book again.

157

Finally, Mama sank down with a sigh in our old wing chair across from the couch. "What's Beryl Ann going to think?" she asked. Then she limply waved her hand, sending me off to my room. She didn't even bother to ground me.

Somehow, her not having the energy to do that and looking so tired and worn out made me sad. More than anything I wanted Mama to be proud of me. But it seemed so hard to be good in the way she wanted me to be. Maybe Mrs. Beaumont was right; kids like me were just plain bad. Maybe there was no getting around it.

Mama was so good, and she worked so hard. She didn't deserve a daughter like me. I wanted to disappear. I curled up into a ball on my bed and cried until I fell asleep.

When I woke up, Grandma was sitting on the end of the bed watching me. "You look like you got chewed up and spit out by a bear," she said.

"Thanks, Grandma," I moaned, stretching and sitting up. For some reason, what she said didn't get my dander up. I crossed my legs and took a few swipes at my crusty eyes with the backs of my hands. My throat was dry and I was having a hard time swallowing. "I need a drink of water."

Grandma got up and soon came back with a tall glass of water. "Here you go," she said. She sat back down and looked at her sandals and then at me. "You run pretty fast."

I smiled. "You shoot pretty good."

Grandma nodded her head. "I used to be a crack shot in my day. Ralph—you may not remember him, he was my second husband—he liked to put up targets in the back yard. We'd practice almost every day. But that stopped when Ralph died."

"Ralph died?" I asked, amazed. "I thought my real grandpa was the only one that died. I thought you divorced all the rest."

"Lordy, no! Ralph and your grandpa both died of natural causes. The others...ah, well. Mistakes." Grandma looked uncomfortable. "Maybe I just divorced the others before they could up and die on me. Who knows? I'm jinxed, I guess."

"Grandma! You're not jinxed! You saved Baby and Dickie today. And you didn't have anything to do with Grandpa Henry dying, or Ralph."

"I know, I know. But people talked, especially after Ralph. He had a heart attack. Some said maybe I ruined his health or wore him out on pupose. Just because there was a little money he left me. Did you ever hear anything so ridiculous?" Grandma paused for a deep breath. "The truth is, I wouldn't have hurt a hair on his head. He was a good man, like your Grandpa Henry."

I couldn't believe it! Grandma was actually talking to me. Maybe I could get some of my questions answered. I grabbed one of her hands. "Grandma, tell me about Grandpa Henry. I've never even seen a picture of him."

Grandma stiffened and took her hand out of mine. "Now, why do you want to bring that up? He's been dead so long. The thing to do is to look to the future."

I was starting to get mad again. I knew any truce with Grandma was going to be a short one, but I'd hoped that for once...just for once....I took a deep breath and stopped myself. I didn't know exactly how to say what I needed to say, but I had to get it said.

159

I closed my eyes and said it as straight as I could. "Because...I don't even know what color Grandpa's eyes were. Because I don't have any history—nothing. Because Lester's got things that have been there forever, but I don't have a grandpa anymore, and I don't have a daddy, either. And I don't have pictures of anybody, except you and Mama. That's why!" I opened my eyes to discover I'd been pounding on the bed with my clenched fist.

When I finally glanced at Grandma, after taking several shaky breaths, she had gone all wide-eyed. "Gracious, girl," she said. "All right, then, we'll talk." She crossed her legs and bounced her yellow-sandaled foot up and down. "You don't have to get hot under the collar about it."

I rolled my eyes at her. Then I settled against my pillows and unfolded my legs.

"Well, first off, your Grandpa Henry had the most beautiful green eyes."

"He did?" I asked, sitting quickly back up.

"Of course he did," she snorted. "Where'd you think yours came from, the Piggly Wiggly? Now, quit interrupting me if you insist on hearing all this."

I sat back, smiling.

"As I was saying before I was so rudely interrupted"— she arched an eyebrow over at me—"he had the most beautiful smiling green eyes. Just like yours. In fact, you're the spitting image of Henry."

"I am?"

Grandma rolled her eyes at me.

twenty-nine

GRANDMA TOLD ME ALL about Grandpa Henry, how he liked to raise African violets and dry his own corn to make popcorn for the local kids, and how he was always repairing things. He'd repaired the old house a hundred times, their old Studebaker, and a strange wooden footstool that was so ugly folks commented upon it. He kept repairing it every time it broke, even though Grandma hated it. It got to be such an ugly "pet" of a thing that she couldn't bring herself to think about throwing it away while he was alive. It was the first thing she tossed out after he died of a ruptured appendix.

The Hiram hospital was just being built, and by the time anyone realized what was wrong, it was too late to repair Grandpa.

Then Grandma told me about losing the house five years after Grandpa died. She said that when the house went up in flames, with all the memories of him that it held, it was like losing Grandpa all over again. She didn't have any good pictures of him herself, just one small tattered snapshot that had been in her pocketbook the night of the fire. She pulled it out of her red leather wallet for me to see.

It had been cut down and was only about two inches square. A happy man in dress slacks, his white shirt open at the neck, had one foot up on the fender of an old car. "He loved that car. A 1941 Mercury coupe," Grandma said, shaking her head. "Until he ran it into the Little Red River one foggy night. Then he went out and bought the Studebaker. I never liked that Studebaker. I couldn't get him to sell it. I even threatened to run it into the river myself!"

Grandma sighed. "But Henry wouldn't have it. He kept fixing that car up. Finally, it got so he was the only one who could drive it. You know, Henry taught me to drive in the Studebaker."

"You drive good," I said.

Grandma laughed. "Well, it looks like I'm going to need a new car now. I don't know if the Thunderbird can be fixed." Then, with a twinkle in her eye, she slapped the bed. "Ha! Maybe I need to go on a scouting trip. What do you think about that?"

"Scouting trip?" I asked. "Like a Girl Scout trip?"

"No. You know, scouting around for a new husband— one with a new car."

"Grandma!" I put both hands over my mouth. "You wouldn't!" I giggled, and she started laughing, too. I realized that I felt comfortable with her, something I couldn't ever remember feeling before.

We were quiet together for a while. It was good. Mr. Perkins, in his glass tank, was awake. He blinked his eyes as his gaze followed Grandma's foot, up and down.

Suddenly, Grandma looked kind of watery-eyed. Never

in a million years would I have believed that my grand-mother knew how to cry. I thought she must be recollecting something. "What is it, Grandma?"

She looked away from me and said in a soft voice, "Lord, what I wouldn't give to have that old footstool back."

That was when I felt it—a sudden shift. It was like the world itself had taken a deep breath, expanded its sides, and opened up to make a little more room for me, for us.

My Grandpa Bovey had had green eyes and loved African violets, kids, popcorn, and fixing things. I *did* have a whole history that had its own place in the wide world. There was a part of me back there just banging its head to get out and be known. And I had a tiny, flashy grandmother who carried it with her wherever she went.

I got up on my knees, scooted across the bed, and hugged Grandma. She sputtered, snorted, and then put her arms around me. "No need to go getting all wally-mushed on me," Grandma said, patting me stiffly. "I have to say, though, that I was proud of how you handled yourself in an emergency, Jessica."

"I was proud of you, too, Grandma. Boy, you nailed that snake, first shot. Bang!" I pretended to sight down a gun.

"That? That was nothing. We Bovey women may be ladies, but we're tough," she said.

"We Bovey women," I whispered. Yes. I was a member of a long line of Bovey women, tough Bovey women, and green-eyed Bovey men like Grandpa Henry. There was a long, long line of Boveys, with me right at the end. I liked that.

When Mama came into my room a little later, Grandma was showing me how to polish my toenails—once she'd made me wash them. There was no way I was going to let her put Rebel Red polish on my fingernails where everyone would be able to see it. Mama shook her head, sighed, and closed the door.

I told Grandma all about Robert and his glasses. And she listened really well for a change. Then she nodded her head, reached into her pocketbook, and gave me four dollars. I told her it was just a loan. I think she would have given it to me, but I insisted that I would pay it back.

Grandma understood about being beholden to folks, even family. She said maybe Robert and I could work it off, that she'd like to have somebody give her car regular washings—once she figured out if she could get the Thunderbird fixed up. She reminded me that you never know who you're going to run into, and it did a girl good to have a shiny car. I clucked my tongue at her.

Then she made me call Mama into my room and tell her about the challenge.

Mama was impressed. "You saved twenty dollars all on your own? And it's for Robert's glasses?"

"Yup, I worked for most of it. Except the five dollars Robert and I won in the raffle. And Grandma loaned me four that I'm going to pay back."

I knew it wasn't right, but I didn't mention that Mr. Henry had wanted me to give some of the money to Baby Blue. In my mind I saw Doyle's face as he slapped Robert, trying to get our raffle money. So I tried not to think about

164

that part at all and added quickly, "I'm going to give it to Miss Woodruff as soon as I see her again. She's trying to get the government to put in the rest of the money through that War on Poverty."

"I see," Mama said. "Does Beryl Ann know about this?"

"No, ma'am. I was just gonna give the money to Miss Woodruff so she can make sure Robert gets his glasses. I was afraid that if I tried to give it to Beryl Ann, she'd be embarrassed and say 'No, thank you.' Or... or Doyle would try to take it away from her."

"I don't think you need to worry about Doyle now. But Beryl Ann likes to do for herself, if she can." Mama thought for a minute. "Everybody needs help once in a while. Lord knows where we'd be without help from our friends," she said.

"I'd like Beryl Ann to know that I don't always cause trouble," I said.

"She doesn't think that," Mama said. "But if this is done through Miss Woodruff, it might be better not to let on where all the money came from. I think Beryl Ann would be more comfortable with that."

In the end, even though Mama was still upset with me for taking Baby to Dickie's house, she said I'd done a good thing about the money for Robert's glasses and that she was proud of me for being so industrious. She told me to be sure to get the money to Miss Woodruff as soon as I could.

I didn't get grounded. But I had to tell Mama where I was going and exactly what I was going to be doing every day. If there was a change of plans, she made me promise about a million times that I would let her or another adult, like Grandma or Lester, know about it.

She said I had to do this for the rest of the summer because I had to earn her trust back. And if I failed even once to do that, she'd have Mrs. Boyd or Grandma over here to baby-sit, like I was five years old again.

So I did the Girl Scout salute, hoping I'd remembered how to do it right, and I promised over and over to be as good as good can be. After that scare with Ol' One Eye, even I was sure that I'd do my best to stay out of trouble.

thirty

SHACKLETON'S VALIANT VOYAGE showed up early one morning a few days later, tossed up against our kitchen door so hard I thought it would dent the screen. Some of the pages were bent over and the cover was a little dirty. But after I wiped it down and bent the pages back, it didn't look too bad.

I had been staying close to home and wasn't up for a whole lot of excitement. Besides, Mama and Beryl Ann had decided that since Doyle wasn't around to help keep an eye on Baby, all of us kids had to come round to whoever was at the Gas & Go every couple of hours and check in with them. Worse than that, we were pretty much confined to Baylor. No playing along the river or up one of the hollers or going into Hiram.

I deserved it, but I didn't think Robert did. So as soon as I could, I went to the Ketchums' to apologize to Robert for getting him confined to Baylor, too. But Robert didn't seem to mind too much.

"That's OK," he said. "I wouldn't like walking to Hiram or playing somewhere unless you were there."

"You don't think I was plain crazy for going after your library book?" I asked.

Robert shook his head. "No. Besides, you were trying to help," he said. "Dickie was the crazy one for playing with his daddy's snake. You were doing what you thought was the right thing to do. Sometimes a person just has to do that."

I smiled. Except for getting mad at me whenever I got grounded, Robert hardly ever made me feel bad.

So the day the book showed up, I was anxious to get it back to him. I took it, and the twenty dollars, over to the Gas & Go.

Mama hadn't let me go to the Weavers' to give the money to Miss Woodruff because she hadn't had any time to go with me. And the Weavers didn't have a telephone. So I had been spending a lot of my time helping Lester at the Gas & Go. I figured Miss Woodruff would stop by sooner or later and I could give her the money. If not, Mama said she would drive me up there as soon as she could. That would be one big thing accomplished. And it was something I was proud of.

I knew Robert would be checking in sometime in the morning, after Beryl Ann had gone off to the Piggly Wiggly. Then I could give him the book.

I stayed at the Gas & Go counter a good part of the day. Around lunchtime Lester went back to his house to get something, and while he was gone, Missy Salyer walked in. I smiled at her as she came through the door. But then I saw DeeDee's blond curls bouncing into view behind Missy.

"Hi, Jessie!" said Missy.

Missy could be OK, when she wasn't bragging. But DeeDee was always impossible to get along with. She didn't say a thing; she just kind of smirked at me over her shoulder and then floated over to the candy racks in a fog of pink and white.

Missy turned toward me and whispered, "Our daddies are at a meeting and Mama made me invite her to the picture show in Bartlettsville. Ugh!" Missy crossed her eyes. I smothered a giggle.

Then I noticed that Mrs. Salyer was waiting by her car out at the gas pump.

"The movies!" I whispered back as I started around the counter. "What are you gonna see?"

"*Born Free.* They're showing it again."

"Boy, I wish I could see that." Then I said loud enough for DeeDee to hear, "I'll be right back." The bells on the door tinkled as I went to pump the gas for Missy's mama.

We never had many gas customers—maybe one or two each day as folks traveled south to Hiram—but I'd grown up knowing how to work the gas pump.

"Why, hello, Jessica," said Mrs. Salyer. She seemed a little surprised to see me. "Are you working today, child?"

"Yes'm. What grade gas do you want, Mrs. Salyer?"

"Premium, Jessica. Please." I had to admit, Mrs. Salyer had some of the very best manners in Beulah County. She was from Mississippi, and now that I wasn't in the scout troop I kind of missed her Deep South accent.

Mrs. Salyer kept looking at me a little strangely as I went about filling her gas tank. I thought maybe she was remem-

169

bering that pomander ball with the dead spiders stuck to it. We hadn't talked much since, and I wondered if I should apologize again. But I figured she'd rather not have to think about spiders any more than she needed to.

I was almost done pumping the gas when Robert and Baby showed up. Mrs. Salyer looked startled. Now, I know that sometimes Baby can look startling if he has dressed himself and Beryl Ann hasn't had a chance to run him down and clean him up. But from what I could see, he really didn't look so messy.

"Hello, Mrs. Salyer," Robert said, offering his hand.

"Why—why—why, hello, Robert," squeaked Mrs. Salyer, pausing and then shaking Robert's hand.

"It's Robert Edison right now," Robert said.

"How...how nice for you," Mrs. Salyer said, clutching her purse.

I rolled my eyes at Robert and tried to warn him with a shake of my head that I didn't think Mrs. Salyer was feeling so well. She really was starting to act very funny. It was not like her to almost forget her manners. I began to wonder if I ought to go get Missy.

"That'll be two dollars, Mrs. Salyer," I said.

She quickly unsnapped her little pale blue purse and paid me. Then she called out toward the store, "Missy! Missy, dahling!"

Robert and Baby and I watched as DeeDee came running and giggling out of the store, trying not to look at us. Missy followed with a very strange, kind of quiet look on her face. Maybe she was mad at DeeDee or still upset about having to go to the movies with her. "See you later," said Missy under her breath as she got into the car.

"Bye!" I waved and walked back to the door with Robert and Baby. "I've got *Shackleton*," I told Robert. "Dickie must have tossed it up on my porch this morning."

"Great!" he said. "Was it damaged?"

"Nah, not much," I answered as I pushed open the door.

When I walked over to the counter to get the library book, I found out why DeeDee had been laughing. There on the counter lay the *Louisville Courier-Journal* and the *Bartlettsville Bugle*. Both were opened to a big article about Beulah County, Kentucky, and a big picture of Baby asleep on Cooch's belly in the dirt with a half-eaten peach in his hand.

Robert came quickly around the counter. "That's Baby," he snapped, and tried to snatch the papers.

"Yeah. Let me read it!" I snapped right back. It was easier for me to read the article out loud than for Robert to try to hold the papers up close to his face. The picture was of Baby Blue, all right.

The article said that everywhere in Beulah County these reporters had traveled there was evidence of the deepest poverty. That President Johnson's War on Poverty was trying to bring relief to the county in terms of jobs, clothing, education, medical attention, and food. Then there was more about the miners in Greasy Ridge.

Finally, it talked about how some communities were helping their own poor by pitching in and seeing that hungry children, at least, got a little to eat. "In one case, Baby

Blue, as he is known locally, doesn't know the whereabouts of his father, and his mother is often away from the home. Local resident Jessica Bovey confirms that he makes the rounds of the neighborhood picking up bread or fruit. Often food is left out for him."

As I read that out loud, and a bit more about Baby's real name and approximate age, the skin on the top of my head started getting red-hot and my cheeks started throbbing. The heat spread all down my throat and over my shoulders until my chest felt like it was shrinking up and getting too small to hold my heart and my lungs. I wanted to scream out before it all got closed in too tight to make a sound.

Beryl Ann wasn't often home because she was out working to make enough money to support her family. And Mr. Birchfield had made Baby sound like some stray dog that the whole neighborhood had decided to help keep alive by giving him table scraps!

I looked up at Robert's face and swallowed hard. His mouth was closed tight and his eyes were swimming behind his glasses.

Baby had pulled over a stool and had climbed up to see the newspapers. "That's me," he said and smiled as he pointed at the picture.

Just then, Lester walked back in. He took one look at us, put on his glasses, gathered up the papers, and started to read. Robert and I stood there like we were nailed to the floor.

"Great balls of fire!" Lester muttered, slamming the papers down with disgust and looking at me over the rim of his glasses.

"I — I never said it that way, Lester," I stuttered, pointing to the paper. "I just said Baby goes in and eats when he's hungry and folks don't mind. Everybody knows that! But the paper makes it sound like...well, they don't make it sound the way I meant it."

"No, I'm sure you didn't mean it this way. The problem is, everyone that doesn't know us here in Baylor is going to take it the wrong way."

Suddenly, Robert seemed to come out of a trance. Lifting Baby off the stool, he turned and marched to the door, saying over his shoulder, "We better go home in case Mama comes back."

"I just saw your mama headed over to Jessie's," said Lester. "I wondered what she was doing home so early. I expect she's talking to Mirabelle about this. You stay here while I go check up on —"

"No," Robert interrupted him. "Mama might need me. I better go."

Lester looked Robert up and down. "OK, Robert. You go see if your mama is all right, son. I'll keep Baby here with me. Jessie —"

"I'm going, too," I said, before Lester could get any further. "I've *got* to, Lester. It's all my fault. I've got to explain to Beryl Ann."

thirty-one

ROBERT DIDN'T SAY A WORD to me as we crossed the road to my house. I practically had to run to keep up with him. "The newspapers, they've got this all wrong—all wrong!" I wished he would say something. "Robert, I'm sorry. I'm so sorry. It's all wrong. I'm sorry."

I pushed the kitchen door open, and we came to an abrupt halt. Mama and Beryl Ann were seated at the table, with the newspapers spread out in front of them. Beryl Ann had her head down on her arms and was just sobbing her heart out. Mama was squeezed up as close to her as she could get on a kitchen chair, and was trying to get her arms all around Beryl Ann.

"What are folks at work going to say?" sobbed Beryl Ann. "I'm so ashamed, so ashamed. How am I gonna show my face..."

"Hush, hush," Mama consoled her. "People don't believe everything that's written in the newspaper. You know that."

"I don't know. And—oh, Lord! Doyle's going to hit the

roof. He...oh, Lord," Beryl Ann shook all over as she cried.

Then Mama noticed us standing silent just inside the door. She gave me a jaw-locked look, but her face softened when she turned to Robert.

"Robert," she said, "your mama's going to be OK. She just needs to cry this out a little bit, honey. She'll be fine soon."

Robert gulped and nodded.

"Can you go over and stay with Lester while your mama and I talk?" Mama went on. "She needs you to take good care of Baby right now. And can you ask Lester to call the Piggly Wiggly and tell them that your mama won't be coming back to work today? Can you do that for me?"

Robert nodded numbly.

Beryl Ann looked up all streaky-eyed and snuffled, "Go stay with Baby. I'll...I'll be all right." Then she got up and, teetering around the table, came over to give Robert a big engulfing Beryl Ann hug. "OK?" They hugged for a long time.

Robert left without saying anything to me. He barely even looked at me.

I opened my mouth to say something, but Mama caught me quickly with a warning glance. "Please, just go to your room, Jessie. I'll be there in a few minutes."

I sat on the edge of my bed, feeling sick to my stomach. I dragged my pink plastic wastebasket over and cradled it between my knees, just in case, and stared blankly at Mr. Perkins. He blinked back at me.

I didn't know what to do. I didn't want people to make

fun of the Ketchums. They were my friends. So what if they were poor? Beryl Ann did her best.

I hadn't thought that my talking with Mr. Birchfield and Mr. Henry was going to turn out like this. I'd explained to them that Baby was just Baby and that his going into people's houses to eat was no big deal. I didn't think they'd really use any of those pictures of him. And even if they did, I'd thought that might be a good thing. Like Lester had said, sometimes the news could get folks riled up to do good things, to help others. But when I'd seen Baby's picture and read the article, it didn't feel right. It didn't feel good.

I started going over and over in my head what I'd said to Mr. Birchfield and Mr. Henry, and what had happened during their visit. I tried to remember it all, exactly like it was. But I got madder and madder as I thought about it. I'd wanted them to write about how exceptional everything was here in Baylor. Instead, this felt like they'd crept up behind me and done something sneaky. And they hadn't even put a picture of Cooch standing on his head in the papers.

After a while, Mama came in. She pushed up on her bangs with one hand like it hurt her to have her hair touching her face. "OK, Jessie," she said, sitting down next to me on the edge of the bed.

"Mama, I never said those things. At least, not the way they came out in the newspapers."

"I know, Jessie. I know you wouldn't have deliberately done that. But tell me exactly what *did* happen and exactly what you *did* say. Start at the beginning."

She already knew about me saving money for Robert's

176

glasses, and that Mr. Henry and Mr. Birchfield had hired me as a guide. I told her about them taking pictures at the Weavers and giving money to Mrs. Weaver. And I told her how Lester had said that sometimes photographers did that so folks would let them take pictures.

I told her about the pictures they'd taken of Cooch and how they had agreed that Cooch was "exceptional," a good example of local color. I told her about meeting Baby coming out of Miss Maybee's house, and how I'd explained to them that the people that lived here in Baylor didn't mind Baby coming through to eat.

Then I had to tell Mama the hardest part—that the money Mr. Henry had given me was to have been shared with Baby, and I hadn't done that. I'd put all the money in with the money for Robert's glasses. "I'm sorry, Mama. I'm so sorry. I should have given it to Beryl Ann, and then she'd have known that they took pictures of Baby, even if Mr. Henry and Mr. Birchfield didn't go to the Piggly Wiggly to find her. But I was afraid Doyle would find out about the money. Besides," I rushed on, "I didn't really think they'd use a picture of Baby. I told them when Baby ate at people's houses, it was OK with everyone."

I looked at Mama, feeling sure she was disappointed in me again. "But the way the paper reported it, it makes Baby sound like a...I don't know...a dog, or something that we all keep around by giving it handouts."

Mama sighed and sat for a long time on the edge of my bed with her elbows on her knees and her head in her hands.

"I'm sorry," I whispered one more time.

Finally, she said, "It was wrong of you to keep all the money, even for a good cause. At least, you should have told Beryl Ann about the reporters." Mama stood up. "And I do see how, if someone wasn't brought up here and didn't know Baby, what you told them might sound a bit peculiar. I can see how it could have got all mixed up in their minds."

"But they should have told me, shouldn't they, that they were gonna put all that in the paper. I thought they were my friends," I said.

"They certainly should have talked to Beryl Ann before they snapped even a single picture of Baby, or to me before they quoted you."

"Do you think something good can happen because of this?" I asked.

Mama tilted her head and looked at me kind of funny-like.

"I mean, Lester said sometimes good people can come and help folks if they get upset enough by what they see in the newspapers," I explained. "And sometimes good things can come out of something bad. Maybe that's all Mr. Birchfield and Mr. Henry were trying to do—to get people riled up in a good way to help with the president's War on Poverty."

"Well," Mama said, "folks around here certainly are going to be riled up. Let's hope it's in a good way. Who knows, maybe more people will donate money or help Miss Woodruff. The problem is, Beryl Ann has to be able to face her friends and the people at the Piggly Wiggly. She doesn't want them to think she's a bad mother."

"She's not! She's a good mother!"

"We both know that, Jessie," Mama said patiently, "but people who don't know her so well might wonder now. They might wonder if she's fit to take care of Robert and Baby."

"Fit? Fit! That's what that social worker, Mr. Ritchey, was going on about." I made a face at Mama. "Robert didn't like him."

"Mr. Ritchey's got a job to do. The state hires him to keep an eye on kids and make sure they're well taken care of, that kind of thing. And now, because of this article in the paper, he'll probably be back to see Beryl Ann."

"Hmmph!" I snorted. "He ought to be snooping over at Dickie's."

Mama's eyes widened and she sucked in on her lower lip. "We'll see about that," she said. She got up to leave. At the bedroom door she turned. "Beryl Ann's still here, if you've got something to say to her."

I knew I had to, but it wasn't going to be easy. "Do I have to tell her about the money for Robert's glasses?" I asked.

"Not right now," Mama said. "We'll talk about that later."

I shuffled down the hall and into the kitchen behind Mama. Beryl Ann was at the sink, wiping down her face with a wet washcloth. She smiled weakly at me.

"I'm sorry, Beryl Ann," I said, trying not to choke up on my words. "I should have told you the reporters took some pictures of Baby. But I never said what the papers said I did, not the way they wrote it."

She sniffed some more and took a long catchy breath. "I know, Jessie Kay. I know you wouldn't...you wouldn't say anything in the world that would be hurtful to Baby or any of us." She put her hand on the back of a chair to steady herself. "I've just got to get through work tomorrow, and the next day. Then it'll get better." She tried to smile her funny, lopsided smile at me. Only it wasn't working so well right now.

I ran to her and threw my arms around her and buried my face in her dress. "You and Mama are the two best mothers in the whole world!"

"Now you've gone and done it, Jessie Kay," Beryl Ann said as she hugged me. "Now I'm crying again."

thirty-two

I TOLD MAMA THE NEXT DAY that I'd like to give back Mr. Henry and Mr. Birchfield's money. But Mama said no. It was meant for a good cause, and no matter what happened, it ought to be used for that. She also said that as soon as she got home from the Gas & Go for lunch that day, we'd drive up to the Weavers' and give it to Miss Woodruff so she could get Robert's glasses arranged for right away.

Besides, from the look on Mama's face, I knew she had some message she wanted Miss Woodruff to pass on to Mr. Henry and Mr. Birchfield.

Mama was all business that morning. As she passed my bedroom door, she shouted at me to make my bed. "And for goodness sake, clean Mr. Perkins's tank—it stinks!"

"OK!" I started yanking at the sheets on my bed. Then I looked at Mr. Perkins. "It's all right, Mr. Perkins," I said, as I lifted him out of his tank and sat him in a shoebox. "She didn't mean it personally. You know there's just no getting around Mama when she's like this."

So I cleaned my room, and Mr. Perkins's, while Mama

worked. I figured some exercise would do us both good, so I went outside and jumped rope to five hundred and made Mr. Perkins jump ten times before I put him back in his clean tank. Then we both had breakfast.

After breakfast I went over to see Lester. I definitely needed another deep-thinking drink from his well.

I stopped on his porch, slid the well cover to the side, and dropped the bucket. After a nice long drink, I whispered, "Ah...the best water in the world." Then I peeked in the screen door. "Lester?"

He was reading at his kitchen table. He pushed a bunch of papers and books aside as I pulled up a chair and plopped my chin in my hand. "Lester, nothing's turning out right. They got everything in the newspaper upside down, and Robert and Beryl Ann are both upset. And Mama's mad."

I put my head down on the table and felt its coolness on my hot cheek. I glanced up at him. "I didn't know they would actually put a picture of Baby in the paper, and I don't think anything good's gonna come of it. Not like those other articles and pictures you talked about."

Lester nodded. "It's easy for things to get out of hand. Here," he said, adjusting his glasses and pulling over a big book and some of the papers on his table. "I dug out that *New York Times* article again last night." I sat up and he showed me the newspaper we'd looked at a couple of weeks before.

I pointed at the picture of the miner and his family. "You said sometimes news like this can make good things happen. What happened yesterday sure wasn't good. Everyone's crying. And I don't know if Robert's ever gonna talk to me again."

Lester peered at the picture in the paper. "There's only one thing wrong with these kinds of articles and pictures," he said.

"What's that?"

"How would you feel if you were the one in the picture?"

I looked again at the ripped underwear and the torn clothes of the kids in the picture and thought about how dirty Baby had looked in the picture he was in. "I guess I should have gotten Baby all dressed up if he was going to have his picture taken," I said.

"But remember, I told you the photographers who take these pictures don't want that. They want the people in the pictures to look like they do every day. That way the world can see how the poor really live."

"If I was poor, I wouldn't want everybody knowing it."

Lester nodded. "That's just it. Folks have got their pride. It's hard to let the whole world see your suffering."

Then he opened the book he had pulled over. Inside were old black-and-white pictures, mostly of poor folks, by photographers named Walker Evans and Dorothea Lange. There were lots of kids and farmers and their wives who looked limp and worn out. It made me feel real sad to see those pictures.

"These are famous photographs," Lester told me. "Some photographers who traveled through the South during the Depression took them. In their day they did a lot of good. These photographers made folks see that we had poor people right here in America who needed help. Then these pictures helped the president decide what to do. Jobs were created for men and women. Whole programs were set up to help people earn a living. That might not have happened without this kind of proof by hard-working photographers and journalists."

I flipped through Lester's book and then looked back at the picture in the newspaper, imagining myself in it. How would I feel knowing that all kinds of strangers and, worse still, neighbors and uppity people like DeeDee and Lorelei were looking at my clothes and house and seeing how poor I was? It suddenly seemed very personal.

"It doesn't feel right, though," I said. "How can it be good if it feels like it isn't anybody's business?"

"Well, that's what some people say," said Lester. "That it's nobody's business, especially if you're the one in the picture."

Now Lester had me going in circles. "I'm confused," I said. "Mr. Henry and Mr. Birchfield paid Mrs. Weaver, and she really needs the money. So that was good. Maybe it's OK, then. Maybe it's OK that folks know we're poor in Baylor and need help. And maybe it's OK if that miner got ten dollars to have his picture taken," I said, and pointed at the picture. "But maybe it's *not* OK if people are so poor that the only way they have to feed their kids is to take money to let others see them like that—not washed up, and in their old clothes and all."

What I was feeling wasn't a pure feeling, like getting really, purely mad. "This has got good parts to it *and* bad parts to it," I said. I looked at Lester, and then laid my head down on the table again. "I don't know what to think."

He smiled. "Don't think you've got to figure it all out, little one," he consoled me. "Folks who are in this position have got to figure out what's best for them—what they can live with. They've got to decide that for themselves. The thing is, now you know how Beryl Ann may be feeling."

"I should have told her about the pictures," I said sadly.

Lester let me scoot over and sit on his lap. He gave me an extra-long hug. "Mr. Henry and Mr. Birchfield are the adults here. *They* should have talked to Beryl Ann," he said. "Or taken the time to find your mama and talk to her. Don't go beating on yourself. Beryl Ann and Mirabelle are right to be upset... at them."

"I think they're gonna get an earful," I said, remembering the state Mama was in when she left this morning.

Lester smiled. "Let's hope it does some good."

thirty-three

AFTER LUNCH, MAMA AND I were about to pull out of the driveway to go to the Weavers' house when I saw a blue station wagon pull into the Ketchums' drive. "That's Mr. Henry," I told Mama. "Miss Woodruff said they were coming back. Maybe she's with them."

"Hmm. Beryl Ann must not have gone in to work today, after all. Let's wait a couple of minutes and then walk over. I've got something to say to those two."

Uh-oh. I almost felt sorry for them.

Mama backed up the car and we went inside. She paced around the kitchen. I mostly tried to stay out of her way.

After about five minutes she said, "Let's go."

Beryl Ann was sitting on the front porch and leaning forward talking with Miss Woodruff. Mr. Henry, with one of his cameras draped around his neck, and Mr. Birchfield stood down at the bottom of the steps acting like they were both on trial. They shifted nervously from foot to foot.

When Mama and I walked up the drive, past Mr. Henry's station wagon and Doyle's hubcaps, to the porch, Mr. Henry and Mr. Birchfield both raised their hands as

though to say hi. I didn't say anything, not even "Howdy."
Seeing them, with their smiles, I got mad. I started counting
right away, trying not to get all balled up inside and blurt
anything out before Mama got a chance to say her piece.

"I'm so sorry, Beryl Ann. I *did* want an article about the
War on Poverty," Miss Woodruff was saying. "But I certainly
didn't expect anything like this. If they'd checked with me
first, I could have told them about Baby Blue and what a
wonderful community Baylor is. Jessie told me all about
Baylor and Baby when I first got here."

"And *you* should have checked with me before quoting
Jessie," Mama said, pointing her finger at Mr. Birchfield and
Mr. Henry.

"We—" Mr. Henry started, but Miss Woodruff didn't let
him finish.

"Won't you let them do a follow-up story on Baby Blue?"
she asked Beryl Ann. "Then people might understand about
what a close-knit community Baylor really is."

"I'm not sure," Beryl Ann said. "Maybe it's better to just
let things die down."

I noticed Robert standing inside the front door listening.
I raised my hand and waved. He looked at me and nodded.
Well, that was better than nothing.

Every time Mr. Henry or Mr. Birchfield tried to get a
word in, Miss Woodruff acted like she had them by their
ears and wouldn't hear of their protests. And Mama lit into
them again. I have to admit, they heard us all out. They
ended up apologizing about a hundred times to Beryl Ann,
and to Mama and me, and even to Miss Woodruff.

Mr. Birchfield and Mr. Henry were willing to do a follow-up article, but they couldn't convince Beryl Ann that it would be a good idea. Neither could Miss Woodruff.

Beryl Ann kept saying that maybe we shouldn't stir things up again. She said that the people who lived here and knew her would know better than to take the newspaper for the gospel truth.

I'm not sure what Mama thought about the idea, because just as they were arguing about this, Beryl Ann rose straight up out of her chair. Everyone paused and turned.

Doyle and Mr. Whitten had come around the corner of the house. Mr. Whitten stood off to one side, smirking. It was Doyle we all stared at. He stood on the path that ran back to the clubhouse with an old double-barreled shotgun raised and aimed at Mr. Henry and Mr. Birchfield.

thirty-four

"GET OFF MY PROPERTY right now!" Doyle said in a steady voice. I couldn't tell if he'd been drinking.

"Whoa! Hey, there!" yelled Mr. Henry and Mr. Birchfield. "We're...we're going right now." They both threw their arms up and started backing slowly away from the porch, trying to avoid the hubcaps while keeping their eyes on Doyle.

Miss Woodruff had sprung up, too. Mama and I stood side by side on the steps. I could feel Mama's hand sliding over to grab mine. We were all as quiet as we could be.

"Doyle!" Beryl Ann said, breaking the silence. "Put that gun down before somebody gets hurt."

Doyle looked up at Beryl Ann on the porch and shook his head. "Can't do it, Beryl Ann. These two"—he nodded over at Mr. Henry and Mr. Birchfield—"and you, Miss Nosy Body," he said, nodding at Miss Woodruff and waving the gun over in our general direction, "I want you *all* off my property before I forget my manners and shoot somebody."

"Quit waving that thing around, Doyle," pleaded Beryl Ann. "You don't know who you could hurt."

I heard Mr. Whitten snicker. He was chewing on a blade of grass like he was enjoying a day at the fair. "No," he said, doing a little fancy step and waving a hand in the air. "Wave it around there some more, Doyle. Make them dance a little."

That meanness just snapped something loose inside me. I yanked my hand out of Mama's and yelled, "This ain't funny, Mr. Whitten!"

"Sure it is!" He laughed. Then he stopped suddenly and glared at me. "Now, shut up, you mongrel. I've had more than enough of you lately." He spit the blade of grass out the side of his mouth.

Mama grabbed my hand again and made a hushing sound. I was hopping mad. But when I looked quickly up at Mama and saw the control in her face, it calmed me right down. For everyone's sake, I couldn't let my anger get the best of me.

I heard Miss Woodruff moving behind me. She was inching her way across the porch.

"You get down from my porch and get going with these two poor excuses for human beings," Doyle said to Miss Woodruff. "I want all three of you off my property now!" He swung the shotgun and aimed it at Mr. Henry and Mr. Birchfield.

As Miss Woodruff scooted past us, she said, "I was just trying to help."

Doyle's whole body stiffened and his face got beet red. "Help? Help?" he sputtered. "All you did, woman, was to *help* get me kicked out of my own house. *Helped* me so I hardly see my boys anymore. And now, with your two buddies here, you've *helped* me and mine become the laughingstock of Beulah County."

Doyle had swung back in our direction. "Hell, woman," he said, "I'm just trying to save what little I've got left from your kind of nosy-body *help!*"

Now I could see Miss Woodruff's face. She had gone all white, her mouth tight.

"Please, Doyle," Beryl Ann begged from up on the porch, "don't do this. There isn't any going back if you hurt somebody."

"What about us, Beryl Ann?" asked Doyle. He lowered the shotgun but kept it pointed in Miss Woodruff's direction. "What about us? What about the shame they've done brought on us? They hurt us; somebody should have to pay for that. They can't just go around making fun of us in front of the whole world like that."

"I know, I know," Beryl Ann answered. "They came to apologize. They didn't mean it the way it turned out."

"And that brat there." Doyle indicated me with the barrel of the shotgun. "What's she doing talking about us so that it gets reported in the papers?"

"Those weren't my words. They mixed them all up," I said.

Mama yanked at my arm again, hushing me. "Doyle," she said, calmly and quietly, "Jessie was misquoted, that's all. She didn't mean any harm."

Mr. Whitten cut in. "'Didn't mean any harm?'" He spit on the ground again. "That girl's been trouble since the day she was born. You should have put her up for adoption, Mirabelle. Any decent woman would have."

Mama stiffened, but she didn't say anything.

Mr. Whitten came sauntering up closer, like he was lord of the kingdom. He looked us over and chuckled under his breath. Then he stopped in front of me, grabbed me by the chin, and twisted and turned my whole head first one way and then the other.

"Hey!" I yelled, pulling my hand out of Mama's and trying to push him away. "Let go. That hurts!"

Mama reached out and sank her fingernails into Mr. Whitten's arm. "Let her go, Curtis," she said through clenched teeth.

Mr. Whitten turned me loose and leered at Mama. I gave him a dirty look and rubbed my jaw where it felt like his grip had bruised me all the way down to the bone.

"So," he said. "You can see the brat's daddy stamped all over her."

What! My stomach suddenly knotted up and hurt like someone had thrown a big rock right into my middle. I heard Mama gasp.

"Didn't think I knew?" I could tell Mr. Whitten was pretending to be surprised. "Couldn't keep something like that to himself, now could he?" he purred real soft-like. "I thought he was just bragging, but I see it now. Maybe I should do some 'reporting' to a few folks myself, eh?"

Did Mr. Whitten know who my daddy was? I looked into Mama's face.

"Shut up, Curtis!" Mama commanded. Mama had gone

steely hard all over. She was looking him right in the eye and not giving an inch.

I wanted to punch him. I wanted to punch him right there in his gut. And I would have, except that Mama had grabbed my hand again. I started counting to myself. Only, for the life of me, I couldn't remember what came after five.

Mr. Whitten leaned forward and whispered something in Mama's ear that I didn't catch. I thought my hand was going to be crushed for sure and that Mama was going to jump right off the ground and fly all over him like a wet cat. If looks could kill, Mr. Whitten would have been pushing up daisies right then and there—and I'd have made a point to stomp on every single one.

Just then, the screen door flew open and banged shut. "Baby, get back inside!" I heard Beryl Ann order. There was more noise behind me. It sounded like Robert had come out, too, and was trying to catch hold of Baby and drag him inside but couldn't. Baby slipped past Beryl Ann and Robert. When he got near us, Mama turned and lunged sideways for him, but he jumped off the steps and, thumb in mouth, started across the yard.

By this time Mr. Henry and Mr. Birchfield had sidled backwards almost to their car. And Miss Woodruff was stopped in the middle of the drive, watching.

Baby walked right up to Doyle. He took his thumb out of his mouth and clamped both his arms around Doyle's leg. "Daddy!" he said.

Doyle still had his shotgun trained on Miss Woodruff. We stared, unable to move, as Baby Blue clung to Doyle.

Then out of the corner of my eye I saw Mr. Henry, way down by his car, slowly start to raise the camera that was hanging from his neck.

Don't, I said to myself. I must have jerked, because Mama turned slightly and saw Mr. Henry, too. She scowled and cleared her throat, like she was trying to draw everyone's attention to herself. "Go back inside, Baby," she coaxed.

It felt like the world's longest minute. Everything was moving in slow motion — slowed right down to the longest, thinnest intake of breath. It even felt like the wind, the sun, and all the insects had stopped what they were doing and were waiting to see what was going to happen next.

The whole time I kept repeating to myself, *Don't do it. Don't do it, Mr. Henry. Put that camera away,* and praying that Doyle and Mr. Whitten wouldn't notice.

Then Doyle shook himself and looked down at Baby clinging to his leg. "Get inside, Baby!"

Baby clamped on tighter. "Daddy, can you come home?"

Doyle looked at us. Now Robert was standing partway down the steps by Mama and me with his hands gripping and twisting the sides of his overalls. "Come and get your brother, Robert," Doyle ordered.

Except for his nervous hands, Robert looked as straight and strong as Mama. He shook his head. "No."

Suddenly, Doyle heaved one great sigh, and like a load was lifted off him, his shoulders drooped and he lowered his gun. "Oh, Baby," he said, putting his hand on top of Baby's pale hair. "What am I gonna do? What am I gonna do?"

To my complete surprise, Doyle squatted, laid his gun

down, and wrapped his arms around Baby. He burst into great choking sobs, muffling his cries against Baby's small chest. "What am I gonna do?"

Then a whole lot started happening at once. It was as if we'd all gulped air at the same time after holding our breath until we'd almost given out. All except Mr. Whitten, who swore and shot Doyle an ugly look as he stomped off.

Beryl Ann and Robert barreled down the steps, almost shoving Mama and me aside to get to Doyle and Baby. The four of them grabbed at each other and started crying.

Miss Woodruff simply sat down, right on her bottom in the dirt. Her blue dress billowed up all around her. Mr. Henry and Mr. Birchfield dropped everything and came running back through the hubcaps to raise her up.

And Mama started shaking all over. With a loud sigh and a shudder, she slumped down on the wood steps and hugged me with both arms. She held me so tight I *still* had trouble breathing. Then she rocked me back and forth. She was shaking so hard I was afraid she'd come apart. It wasn't easy, but I held on.

When Mama's shakes had subsided enough that she could walk, we went down the drive and made sure Miss Woodruff was going to be all right. Then Mama went in the house and called the county sheriff. We waited until Officer Boyd showed up to arrest Doyle. Then we walked home with our arms around each other.

The next day Mama told me Beryl Ann had called. Doyle would stay in jail until his case came up before the judge.

They'd hauled Mr. Whitten in, too. And Miss Woodruff, Mr. Henry, and Mr. Birchfield had to go in to be questioned. Even Mama had to go to the station.

The sheriff didn't keep Mr. Whitten in custody because he said he had just gone along with Doyle to try to keep him out of trouble. But Officer Boyd knew he wasn't telling the truth. He told Mr. Whitten that he had his eye on him. If Mr. Whitten so much as glanced in the direction of his whiskey still, or took off up to the handler's church to do any more worshiping with snakes, or even so much as spit on a Sunday, Officer Boyd said he'd be more than happy to find a bunk in the jail for him for a good long time.

thirty-five

I STARTED HAVING BAD DREAMS. I'd wake up shaking, or crying out in my sleep. I was tired and cranky.

I spent a lot of time at Lester's. What I needed from Lester right now I couldn't get from Mama. She was acting strangely, almost like she was avoiding me. I knew it had to do with what Mr. Whitten had said. I knew it had to do with my daddy. But I didn't know how to talk to her about it. And I didn't think I could talk with Grandma about it.

When I told Lester that Mama seemed nervous around me lately, he sighed and hugged me. "Give her some time," he said. "She has something to tell you that isn't going to be easy for her."

"Is it about my daddy?" I asked him.

"That's her story to tell, little one, not mine," he said, and hugged me again.

One night after I woke up from a bad dream, Mama was sitting on the edge of my bed. She leaned over and brushed back my hair. "Shh, shh," she whispered. "It's all right, sweetie. It was just a bad dream. It'll go away. Shh, light of my life."

I reached out and took her by the wrist. "Mama, I keep

dreaming about Mr. Whitten. He's like a big old snake hissing ugly things at us. And I'm so scared."

"Oh, sweetie," Mama said. "I would never let anyone hurt you. Not Curtis Whitten, not anyone."

"I know. But he *did* say something to you that hurt *you*. What did he mean?" I looked at Mama, gripping her wrist tighter. "He knows who my daddy is, doesn't he?"

Mama looked away and started to rise from the bed. "It's late, honey. You should go back to sleep."

I held onto her wrist and sat up. "Please?"

"Tonight?"

"Please, Mama. I've got to know sooner or later, and it *is* about me. I *should* know," I pleaded. "If you don't tell me... I don't know what will happen. I keep dreaming that Mr. Whitten is whispering things — bad things. He's telling everybody, and people are laughing."

"You're right," she said. She wiggled her wrist free from my grasp and rubbed it. I didn't know I'd been holding on so tightly. She brushed her hand lightly across my cheek. "You need to hear it from me. But it isn't a pretty story, Jessie," she warned.

"That's OK," I told her, even though I was a little scared. Deep down I'd always known something was wrong from the way Mama acted — sad or angry or impatient — when I asked about my daddy. I just knew I had to hear it right now, tonight, and I hoped it wasn't too bad. "I need to hear it anyhow," I said.

Mama whispered, "Oh, love, you are the light of my life."

She paused for a long time after that. It took her so long

to get started I thought she'd forgotten what she was going to do. "Mama?"

"Let's see." She cleared her throat and sat up straighter. "You remember, I told you about the bad times and the house burning down?"

I nodded.

"Well, something happened before that, before the house burned down. I..." Her voice trailed off. "I...Well, you're a big girl. And..."

I knew all about how babies are made, what Grandma calls "the birds and the bees." "Did you fall in love with someone?" I asked. Even though all the faces of my pretend fathers through the years had been kind of blurry, I'd often imagined Mama falling in love with someone and being happy. For a long time I'd hoped that it had been Warren.

"No, no," Mama whispered and looked down. "That was the problem. I, ah...I didn't love your father at all."

I didn't understand. "You didn't? Then why...?"

Mama looked at me, and there were tears in her eyes. She took a big swipe at them. "I didn't want to....Oh, Jessie, honey, I don't want to hurt you and spoil whatever you've imagined about this. But, honey, it was bad. He forced me to. I..." Mama stopped and took a deep breath.

I tried to take it all in. My eyes hurt from straining forward, trying to understand what she was saying.

She continued, "It was after I became friends with Warren. I went with him to a conference in Owensboro. I was young and excited. I talked about it a lot. I was going to observe at my first medical conference. Traveling all those hours to Owensboro and back, just Warren and I. Folks heard about it and didn't like it."

Mama stared down at her shaking hands and clenched them together. "Someone—a bad man—wanted to teach me a lesson. Someone I knew, but I never thought he'd..." She swung her head from side to side like she was trying to fling away an ugly picture. "We'd known each other since we were kids. And even though we didn't like each other, I just never thought he'd actually hurt me like that. He...he forced himself on me, Jessie."

While Mama paused and put her face in her hands, I tried to make sense of it. My thoughts kept running up against a big dark wall. I'd thought it might be a sad story Mama was going to tell me, but I'd never thought it was going to be this bad.

Slowly I slid my hands up to the sides of my head to cover my ears. But I knew I had to hear the rest. I couldn't go back to my imaginings anymore, it wouldn't be the same. It was like the clubhouse, only much, much worse.

"I don't understand, Mama," I whispered, not wanting to understand.

When Mama raised her face, tears were streaming down her cheeks. "I'm sorry, Jessie. It wasn't about love or romance or any of those good things. It was all about being angry and hitting, and someone bigger and stronger than me wanting to hurt me. I...I went to Warren afterward, since he's a doctor. He helped me. He wanted me to go right to the police. He would have gone himself and filed a complaint, but I stopped him."

"Why? *Why?*" I yelled, finally finding my voice and letting my hands drop from my ears. My stomach knotted up, and I could feel the heat beginning to spread all over me. I didn't bother with trying to calm myself down. Someone had hurt Mama, and she hadn't even complained about it! "Why not?" I asked, clenching up a fistful of blankets.

Grandma had said that we Bovey women are tough and strong. I had to know why she hadn't stood up for herself, hadn't even bothered to go to the police. "Why?" I demanded again.

"I was scared, Jessie. He threatened to hurt us if I told. He told me he'd hurt Grandma. And then . . . and then a couple of months later the house burned down. I knew he'd done it. It was a warning to keep my mouth shut. I was so scared." Mama looked around the room and then back at me. "I wanted to go, to run away. But there wasn't any place to run to. After the fire, there was no money to run with. And then . . . he died, and I didn't need to run. He couldn't hurt us anymore.

"Oh, Jessie," Mama whispered, reaching out to stroke my arm. "You don't know how much I hoped and prayed that I could avoid telling you this. I hoped that somehow, it'd all . . . I don't know—I guess I was hoping it would just melt away as you grew up, and it'd be all right if you never knew the whole story. But I've known that I was fooling myself, ever since that day at the Ketchums'. I knew that I'd have to tell you, or Curtis might."

I could tell that Mama was trying to smooth it all out for me. But it still didn't make sense, not if the man who'd hurt

Mama was dead now. "If he couldn't hurt us anymore, why'd you keep it a secret?"

"After that, what did it matter?" Mama asked. "We were all finally safe. And I didn't want people talking about me even more. Also … there were others who would have been hurt by knowing the truth. I just wanted to live unafraid again. I didn't want to think about it anymore."

"Who didn't you want to hurt, Mama?"

She tilted her head and stroked my cheek. "Most importantly, you. I didn't want the child I was carrying to ever, *ever*, be ashamed of who she was."

I closed my eyes, leaned forward, and hid against her, thinking. After a while, I asked, "Who else would have been hurt?"

Mama sighed. "Lester."

"Lester!" I yelped, falling back on my pillow. I was more confused than ever. "What does *he* have to do with it?"

"Lester had already had a lot of sadness in his life. Darlene, his daughter, was as good as gone; nobody had heard from her in years. His wife had died not too long before this. I didn't want to hurt him again."

"But I still don't understand about Lester, Mama."

"Lester's grandson—Jack. He was the one." Mama heaved a body-shuddering sigh.

"Jack?" I whispered. I could feel my stomach and back tensing up. "You mean the one in the picture in Lester's living room?"

"Yes. Darlene's son."

I tucked my knees up into my chest and laid my head

down so my eyes were shut up tight against my knees. I pushed into my kneecaps, trying to black everything out, hoping that when I looked up again I could see it all straight and lined up instead of all crazy and scattered.

I didn't say anything for the longest time. Finally, I looked up. "Jack... forced you?"

"Yes." Mama sighed again.

"He's the one? He's my... *father?* And you never said so, even after he died, so Lester wouldn't get hurt?"

"Yes." Mama nodded. "And to protect you. I never wanted you to know this, Jessie.

"As for Lester," Mama spread her hands out and continued, "you know, Lester's been like a father to me ever since my own daddy died. I didn't want him to know how bad, how... well, what a bad person his only grandchild was."

Then she turned to avoid my eyes. "I never even told Grandma," she whispered. "She wanted me to tell her, so she could... I guess, somehow make it better—to insist that whoever had gotten me pregnant should marry me. But I couldn't. I didn't want that! I wanted it to all go away. I was just living from day to day and hoping something would happen to change things. And then one night it did."

There was another long pause, while Mama seemed to be remembering. "Jack and Curtis were friends. One night they were out drinking. They took the hairpin curve down the other side of Martin's Mountain too fast and flipped Jack's car. The sheriff said it must have rolled at least seven times down over the side of the mountain until it landed up against a tree, partway down."

Mama was staring silently off into space again. I nudged her arm a little. "What happened?"

"Curtis got thrown free right away, they said. But Jack got pinned between a tree and the car. He lived for a couple of days in the Hiram hospital."

Mama shook herself and continued. "And even though Lester was disappointed in his grandson, it hurt him badly. Lester had hopes—hopes that Jack would straighten up and become someone he could be proud of. I don't think Lester knew what kind of person Jack really was. After Jack died, Lester's hopes were all gone—all of his family, gone," Mama said, spreading her hands wide. "Not one left.

"So I never said anything. He'd been through enough. Besides, Lester knew I couldn't stand Jack. Jack and I had never liked each other. He was a bully. If I had told Lester that Jack was your father, he'd have guessed the truth about how it happened. And I didn't want to talk about it or think about it again. I wanted us all to just get on with our lives."

Mama watched me intently, her tired eyes on my face. One thing she'd said kept coming back into my head. She'd wanted it all to go away.

"Mama," I asked, "do you wish it had never happened?" I swallowed hard. "Do you wish that I wasn't here?"

Mama jumped back like I'd hit her. "Oh, God, Jessie! Sweetie!" she said. She steadied herself and took another deep breath. "I wish it had happened differently. Yes. Yes, I *do* wish that. But..." She grabbed me by both shoulders, pulled me up so we were face to face, and said, "I love you. You are, and will always be, the light of my life."

I started to cry. "Are you glad I was born, Mama?"

"Glad? Glad?" Mama said. She wrapped her arms around me and hugged me to her chest. "Oh, Jessie, *glad* isn't the right word. There isn't a second of my life—not one second—that I'm not thankful with every ounce of my being that you came into my life."

"Really?"

"Really." Then she kissed me and crawled under the covers with me. All night I slept in my mother's arms.

thirty-six

THE NEXT MORNING I woke up before Mama. She was on her side, one foot sticking out from the sheets, her toe almost touching Mr. Perkins's tank. I crept out of bed, went to the bathroom, and came back. Mama looked tiny lying in my bed, like she wasn't much older than me. I let her sleep.

I tiptoed down the hall and into the living room. I pulled back the curtains and looked over at Lester's house. Early this morning it had dawned on me that Lester must be my great-grandpa.

It was strange to realize that I had a whole other family. And Lester's house with its history and his things—now they were my history, too. My fingertips tingled. I wanted to go right over there and make my rounds.

That seemed like a good thing. And then I thought about the bad part of it. I had that same uneasy feeling I'd had a lot lately, like I didn't know whether to feel good or bad.

All my life I had wished that Mama had married my father so I could have a daddy at home like everybody else. And all my life I had wondered why she always seemed sad when I asked about him and why she didn't want to talk about him. Now I knew why.

Now I was glad Mama had never married him. He would not have been a good father. He was not a good person. He had hit her and hurt her. Thinking about that made me mad; so mad I wanted to hit something myself.

I wondered if that part of me that was always so mad came from my father. Maybe Mama was wrong, and Grandma and I *weren't* two peas in a pod. Maybe part of me was angry and just plain bad, and I'd gotten that from him. Maybe Mrs. Beaumont was right—that I was never gonna get into heaven, anyway. My stomach felt funny. It was too hard to think about.

Then I remembered that Mama had been strong. She'd stayed here with Lester, even when no one knew the truth and people had gossiped about her. And now I had a great-grandpa and a whole other history. Lester was my great-grandpa! That made me smile.

I got very lightheaded. All of a sudden, it seemed like there was a whole lot more of me in the world. It was like after Grandma had told me about Grandpa Henry and the world had welcomed me and said, "It's OK, there's room for every little bit of you."

While I was standing there staring at Lester's house, Mama came into the room. She put her hand on my shoulder. "Are you all right?" she asked.

"Yes," I said and looked up at her. "Lester's my great-grandpa."

"That's right."

"Are you sure he doesn't know?" I asked.

"I don't think so. I never told him. Why?"

"Well, the other day he said something strange to me. He said that you had something to tell me that wasn't going to be easy."

"What?" Mama looked surprised. She chewed on her lower lip as she looked at me. "Hmm." She took my chin in her hand and studied me. "Maybe..." she mused. "Maybe. Lester's old, but he's as sharp as a tack. What *should* we do about Lester?"

"And Grandma," I said.

"Grandma?" Mama asked. "Yes, you're right. I need to have a talk with Grandma, too. I owe her that." Mama hugged me. "Sometimes you amaze me, Jessie."

"Can I be the one to tell Lester?"

"I don't know. It's been a long time," Mama said. "Let's not jump into things. I tell you what. Let's eat first; I'm starved. Then we can think about it together."

We decided that both of us would go over to visit Lester before Mama went to work. But Mama insisted that I wasn't to blurt anything out until she saw the lay of the land and made sure Lester was OK.

Mama took Lester some of the biscuits I'd helped make that morning. While the two of them stood in the kitchen talking, I made my way into the living room. I touched Lester's books, his pipes, his wife's figurines, and his pictures—all with just the tip of my finger. They felt new and familiar at the same time. Lester, the wonderful person he was, was mine! My Lester. *My* great-grandpa. Nobody could take that away from me, ever.

When I came to the black-and-white photograph of Jack, I picked it up and studied it. His mouth was somehow familiar, but not friendly. His eyes looked brittle, like they'd shatter if he blinked. My stomach did a queasy flip. Now I knew why I'd never liked this picture. I set it back down quickly and turned toward the kitchen.

Mama and Lester were watching me. Lester smiled. "It seems like you two have got something to say," he said. "Maybe we all need a drink from the well?"

We went out on the porch, and Lester hauled up a bucket of water. We dipped in and passed the cold, wet ladle around.

Lester waited as Mama drank, and then me. When I'd finished, I put my arms around him and hugged him. "The best water in the world," I said.

"Yes," Mama agreed. "The best water in the world."

Lester brushed his knobby hand over my head. He turned and took a good swig of well water himself. "Best water in the world," he said.

"I love you," I whispered.

"Why, you whippersnapper you—I love you, too, and always have," he said. "From the first minute your mama brought you squealing and squawking into my house. I remember saying to her, *Mirabelle, what in the world am I going to do with this little firecracker?*"

"You did?"

"Yup. And you know what your mama did? She laughed. Yes, sir. That was the first I'd heard her laugh in a long

209

time . . . a very long time." Lester sighed. "And you know what I thought?"

"What?" I asked.

"I thought, Lester, you old lucky dog you, you've got another chance. This girl has brought me a great-grandbaby."

"What?" Mama squeaked, falling back against the side of the house. "Lester, how in the world . . ."

"You didn't!" I said, hugging him tighter.

"I sure did," he said. "I could tell by the way that wide mouth of yours was hitched up to one side and screaming that you had Jack's temper."

I made an ugly face at the mention of Jack's name. "Mama says I've got Grandma's temper. And Grandma says I'm the spitting image of Grandpa Henry."

Lester raised an eyebrow and nodded his head. "Well, they're right. You *are* the spitting image of Henry. And as to Anna Mae's temper, well, let's just say I'd much rather see that in you than anything of Jack's. He wasn't worth a plug nickel. Always knew it in my bones. I tried to blame it on that no-account husband of Darlene's that up and left when he was little. Fool that I was, I kept hoping he'd straighten up. But then he started going around with Curtis Whitten. Bad stuff they got into. I should have run him off, even if he was my own kin."

Then Lester looked at Mama and reached over to put his hand on her shoulder. "Forgive me, Mirabelle," he said. "I tried not to think about what kind of a person he was back then. I was an old fool. I'm sorry if he . . . well, I'm sorry that he hurt you, Mirabelle."

Mama started to say something but stopped. Then she buried her face in her hands and cried. Lester and I both put our arms around her and held her for a long time.

After a while Lester looked over at me. He said, "The important thing, Jessie, is that you've got your mama's heart and strength."

"And Grandpa Henry's green eyes," I added.

"Yes," said Mama, breaking free of us and wiping at her face. "And Lester's...I don't know what. Lester's..."

"My dancing ability?" Lester asked her with a smile. Then he rubbed his hands together. "I don't know about you two, but I'm feeling pretty spry all of a sudden. Who knows, maybe I'll go out tonight and get me a fancy woman and go dancing. What do you think?"

"Lester!" Mama pretended to be scandalized.

"On the other hand," he said, wrapping us both up in his arms again, "maybe we could just have us a *family* dinner after work tonight. I'd like to have dinner with my great-granddaughter."

"Yes!" I said. "And with Mama, too?"

"Of course. She's my...well, what can we say? Mira-belle's always felt like a granddaughter to me. Will you be my honorary granddaughter?" he asked Mama.

"I am, and have been since I was a little girl," she said, and kissed his cheek.

"What about Grandma?" I asked. "Is she part of this family, too?"

Lester shook his head and laughed. "I'm not sure I'm prepared to go *that* far!"

thirty-seven

I GAVE THE MONEY I'd saved to Miss Woodruff, and she got the government to come through with their part. So Robert finally got his glasses. I was really happy about that. Mama and Lester were proud of me. But Grandma was the best. She just snorted and said she never doubted I could do it. "You're a Bovey, aren't you?" she said. Now I just have to work off the loan—as soon as she gets a new car I can wash.

We never said anything to Beryl Ann about me raising the money. Mama said sometimes just the doing of a thing is its own reward, and I know she's right. Oh, sure, Robert still has to hold books and papers up high to read them, but not *as* high. And he doesn't squint as much either. Miss Woodruff is looking into getting Robert to a specialist in Lexington to see if anything else can be done for him. I'm keeping my fingers crossed.

School has started up again. Unfortunately, we don't have Mr. Prichard this year. But we do have Mrs. Winters. She's new. I don't think she's too impressed with DeeDee or

Lorelei. She's already scolded them for talking in class and makes them sit far apart. I turned around in my seat and crossed my eyes at Lorelei when she told Mrs. Winters she was going to complain to her father the mayor about the seating arrangements. Mrs. Winters just smiled and said, "You may go ahead and do that, Miss McMasters. But in this class we are all equal, and we will behave that way."

As it turned out, the folks around here were pretty divided about the first newspaper article. When Baylor made the headlines *again,* about the showdown at the Ketchums', people were still divided. Some said that a man had a right to protect his family. And they said the president's War on Poverty was just an excuse to go snooping around in the private business of others, that it wasn't much better than revenuers coming around looking for whiskey stills.

But other folks thought a lot of good was getting done. Baby and many of the younger kids got into Head Start, and the miners' kids got medicines and new clothes. A class for grownups who wanted to finish high school started, too. None of that could have happened in Beulah County without someone like Miss Woodruff coming here.

Doyle has to stay in jail a while longer. Mama told me it wasn't as bad as it sounded because Doyle said he wanted help with his drinking. She said that Mr. Ritchey, the social worker, was going to help Doyle arrange it. I guess Mr. Ritchey isn't as bad as I'd thought, either.

And we all heard that Mr. Ritchey made some trips up Dog Gap to the Whitten place. Not too long ago Dickie and

Mrs. Whitten packed their bags and moved in with Dickie's aunt. I was glad for Dickie, though I knew we'd never like each other. Adam was right. No kid deserved Mr. Whitten as a father.

Mr. Henry and Mr. Birchfield took off out of town as soon as they could. Miss Woodruff stayed. She's a tough one. The people down here like that. She even got a men's civic group in Cincinnati to donate a new coffeepot for the church! Mr. Dutton was very pleased.

On Baby's first day of Head Start, he was scrubbed clean and wearing polished shoes from the Salvation Army store. He even had a part slicked down in his hair. I was proud of him as Beryl Ann and Robert marched him to school, but I was worried, too. I was afraid he might pick up someone's snack and eat it himself, or he might wander out of the schoolroom or bring a snake inside—things like that. But Mama said not to worry. She said the teachers know about Baby Blue and how wonderfully "exceptional" he is. Mama was right. I didn't need to worry. Baby is a favorite of the Head Start teacher, and he's learning to read already.

I worry a little about Robert, also. All the kids for miles around know Doyle's in jail. They all know about Baby and how poor the Ketchums are. But it's true: Robert is brave. He just ignores any taunts from the kids at school.

He's talking to me again, and helping me with my homework. With the new glasses, that's a little easier. But since Doyle got arrested and school started, we haven't done much at the clubhouse. The other day I walked in and found him there putting a picture of Sir Edmund Hillary, the famous mountain climber, on the wall. "*He's* not a movie star," I said.

"So?" Robert shrugged. "It's dopey to stick with movie stars only. I thought we could branch out."

Robert started using Edmund for a middle name, but I don't know how long he'll keep it. Just yesterday Mrs. Winters was talking about President Harry S. Truman, and when Robert asked what the "S" stood for, she smiled and said, "S." Later I saw Robert with a library book about the president.

Also, he checked out a book for me about a famous aviator, Amelia Earhart. "I like reading about Amelia Earhart," I told him while we were in the clubhouse.

"That's good. I thought you would," he said, and sat down on the chair Mama had repaired.

I sat down on the cooler and stared up at the picture of Sir Edmund. "Do you think he ever did anything bad in his life?" I asked. "Or Amelia Earhart—did she ever do anything bad?"

"Probably," Robert said. "Most people have done some bad things in their lives."

"Yeah, but what if they were born with some *really* bad stuff in them? Do you think they'd still be able to do good things? I mean, that badness has to come out somehow, doesn't it? Even if you climbed a mountain or tried to fly around the world, one day it could just sneak up on you."

Robert looked at me kind of strange-like. "It doesn't work that way. First off, what you're born with don't matter that much. Mama says you do the best you can and start fresh each day."

I could picture Beryl Ann saying that. "You mean, you don't think some people are gonna end up in hell just because, well...because they got bad blood in them?"

Robert frowned and leaned forward. "Are you afraid you got bad blood?"

I lifted my foot and picked at the label on my sneaker. I couldn't look at him. "I could have," I whispered.

"That's hogwash, Jessie," he said, sounding angry. "I know who my daddy is, and he *did* do something bad. But I don't think he's gonna go to hell. And I don't think I am either, just because I got his blood in me! It don't matter whether you know your daddy or not, or if he ever did bad things, Jessie. All that matters is what you do. Besides"— Robert sat back and touched his new glasses—"you're my friend. And even if you do lose your temper once in a while, I think you're a good person."

"You do?" I asked.

"Of course."

I smiled and looked around at our collection. "I'd put Amelia Earhart's picture up, too, if I could find one to cut out."

"Maybe we could send away for one," he said.

Robert was right; we needed to branch out.

Missy has been over a few times to visit. I found out that her daddy won't let her have any pets at all. That hardly seems fair. So I let her hold Mr. Perkins whenever she wants.

We were going through the Sears and Roebuck wish book the other day, and I told Missy about the bra Grandma bought me. She says she has one, too. We decided it might not be so bad if we both wear ours on the same day.

But I have to wash mine out good first. I was trying to teach Mr. Perkins to do somersaults and the bra made a good trampoline. Only he didn't feel like jumping. He just sat on it and peed.

Some things are still the same. I still get mad. But now I stop and remember Mr. Whitten all red in the face when he saw that Ol' One Eye was dead, or Doyle, mad and just kind of flinging that gun around. When I think of those things, I can usually simmer right down. If not, I still count—sometimes. Or I think about Robert and how calm he stays, and I try to do the same. I've even got something helpful to say if DeeDee or Lorelei ever makes me mad again. I'll say, "You'd look better without cotton balls stuffed in your bras."

Last night while Mama was doing supper dishes, there was a knock on the kitchen door. Mr. Perkins and I were in the hallway. I picked him up and we peeked around the corner to see who had come.

Adam was there with his cap in his hand. He kept turning it around and around, like he couldn't decide which was the right way to hold it. Every so often he'd glance down and act surprised that he had it in his hands instead of on his head. It was funny to see him so nervous.

Adam asked Mama to go out to the Roadside Grill! I sucked in my cheeks and slid down to sit on the floor. *Say yes... say yes... say yes... say yes,* I started repeating to myself. *Please, please, Mama, say yes!*

It seemed to take her forever to answer him. Mr. Perkins

and I were very still, waiting to hear her answer. We had almost given up on her, when Mama said, "Yes, I'd like that very much."

When I walked into the kitchen a little later, Mama was sitting at the table with a kind of dazed and happy look on her face. I sat down and tapped my fingernails on the table-top. I figured now was a pretty good time to ask Mama's permission for something I wanted to do.

I cleared my throat and said, "Grandma asked me if I wanted to go to Nashville with her over Christmas break."

"She did?" Mama asked. "What are you going to do there?"

"Grandma said it was a scouting trip."

"Oh, Lord," Mama sighed.